EXCEL 2024

From Novice to Mastery in 6 Days: Harnessing Advanced Techniques, Practical Insights, and Expert Secrets to Rapidly Elevate Your Skills.
4 Exclusive Bonuses Included!.

By Vincent Fairmont

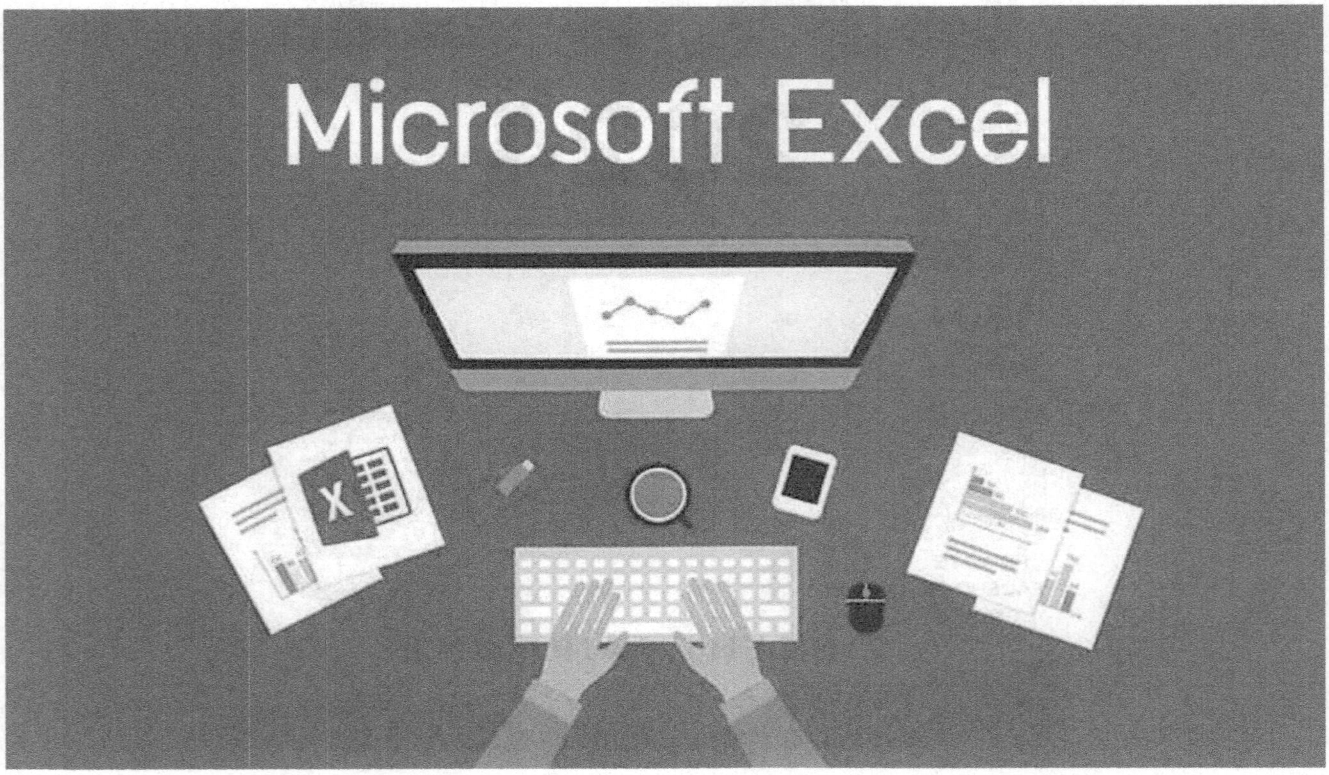
Microsoft Excel

LEAVE A REVIEW & GET REWARDED!

Don't wait! Scan the QR Code and **CLAIM YOUR EXCLUSIVE FREE BONUSES!**

SCAN ME

1.1 What is Excel 2023

Microsoft Excel 2023 is the latest version of Microsoft's widely used spreadsheet program. As part of the Microsoft Office suite, Excel is used by millions of individuals and businesses worldwide for various tasks, ranging from simple data entry and accounting to complex data analysis, visualizations, and decision-making tasks.

At its core, Excel is a grid of cells organized in rows and columns. Each cell can contain numerical or textual data or the results of formulas that automatically calculate and display values based on the contents of other cells. It's a versatile tool that can handle everything from simple arithmetic to complex statistical and engineering calculations.

In addition to its powerful calculation abilities, Excel 2023 offers many features that help manage and manipulate data. You can sort and filter lists of data, create visually appealing charts and graphs, and use a wide array of formatting options to make your spreadsheets easy to understand and pleasing to the eye.

1.2 What's New in Excel 2023

Every new version of Excel brings enhancements, new features, and improvements, and Excel 2023 is no exception. The 2023 version introduces several notable updates that make it even more powerful and user-friendly.

1. **Improved Collaboration**: The collaboration tools in Excel 2023 have been significantly improved, allowing for better real-time collaboration. This means multiple people can work on the same spreadsheet at the same time without the risk of overwriting each other's changes.
2. **Data Types**: Excel 2023 introduces new data types that go beyond numbers and text. These data types include Stocks and Geography, and

they can automatically associate rich, structured data from the internet to the related entities.

3. **Dynamic Arrays**: This new feature changes how Excel handles arrays, allowing single formulae to output (spill) values to multiple cells.

4. **XLOOKUP Function**: XLOOKUP is a new function that replaces the older VLOOKUP and HLOOKUP functions. It's simpler, more flexible, and corrects many of the limitations of its predecessors.

5. **LET Function**: This function allows you to assign names to calculation results. This makes formulas easier to read, write, and understand.

These are just a few of the new features and improvements in Excel 2023. This book will cover these and many other features in detail throughout the chapters.

1.3 Installation and Setup

Before you start using Excel 2023, install it on your computer. Excel 2023 is part of the Microsoft Office 2023 suite, including other productivity tools like Word, PowerPoint, and Outlook.

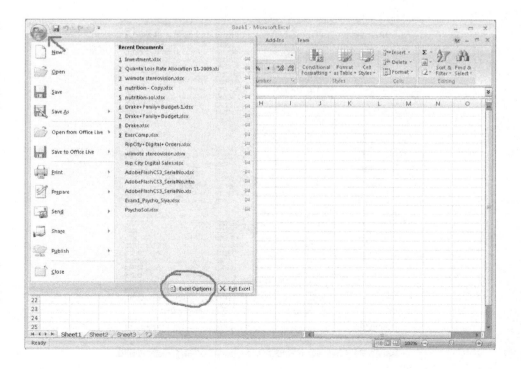

To install Office 2023, follow these steps:

1. **Purchase Office 2023**: You can purchase it directly from the Microsoft website or from a retail store.

2. **Download and Install**: Once you've purchased Office 2023, you can download the setup file from the Microsoft website. Double-click the setup file and follow the on-screen instructions to install Office 2023 on your computer.

3. **Activate Office 2023**: After the installation is complete, open any Office app, such as Word or Excel, and you'll be prompted to activate Office. You can

1.6 Excel Shortcuts

Knowing your way around Excel shortcuts can significantly speed up your work in Excel. We'll review some of the most essential shortcuts for navigating, entering data, and working with formulas.

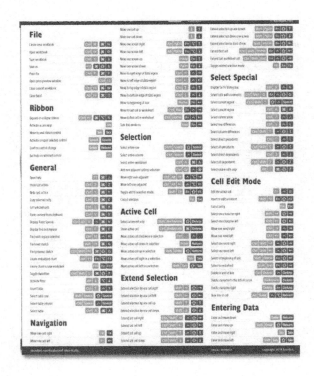

1.7 Customizing the Excel Interface

Excel allows you to tailor the interface to your needs. Learn how to customize the Quick Access Toolbar and Ribbon, change Excel's color scheme and theme, and set your default font and number formats.

1.8 Excel Options and Settings

There's more to Excel's customization than just the interface. Delve into the backstage view to set Excel options like formula calculation settings, AutoRecover options, and language settings.

1.9 Using Excel Templates

Save time by starting with an Excel template for your task, whether it's a budget, invoice, calendar, or project plan. We'll also cover how to create your own templates for tasks you frequently do.

1.10 Excel Help and Resources

When you're stuck or want to learn something new, there are plenty of resources available. We'll introduce Microsoft's built-in Help feature, Excel's community forums, and other online resources to further your Excel knowledge.

1.11 Understanding Excel File Formats

Excel supports several file formats, each with its unique properties. The default format, .xlsx, stands for "Excel Workbook" and it is useful for most common tasks. It doesn't support macros, for which you would need the .xlsm format ("Excel Macro-Enabled Workbook"). Older Excel versions use the .xls format. If you want to save only the current worksheet instead of the whole workbook, you can use .xlsb ("Excel Binary Workbook").

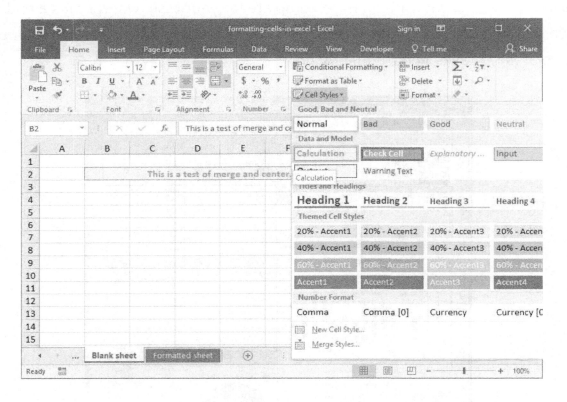

A .csv file ("Comma Separated Values") is a plain text file that contains a list of data. These files are often used for importing and exporting data between different types of software.

1.12 Basic Text and Number Formatting

Excel provides numerous options for formatting text and numbers. To align text within a cell, select the cell(s) you want to format, then in the Home tab, find the Alignment group. Here, you can center text, align it to the left or right, or adjust vertical alignment. For number formatting, you can choose from general, number, currency, accounting, short date, long date, time, percentage, fraction, scientific, and text by right-clicking a cell and choosing "Format Cells", then "Number".

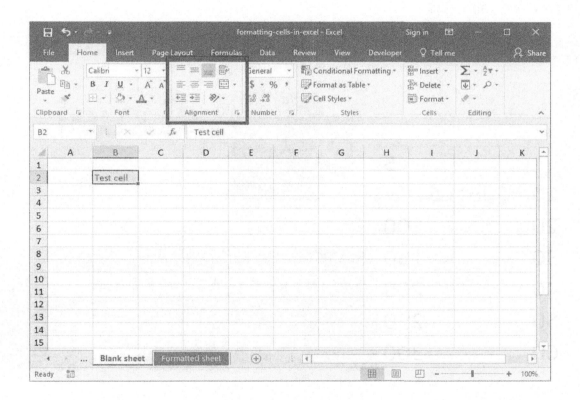

1.13 Basic Conditional Formatting

Conditional formatting allows you to automatically apply formattings—such as colors, icons, and data bars—to one or more cells based on the cell value. To use it, select the cells you want to format, go to the Home tab, and click "Conditional Formatting". Here you can highlight cell rules, top/bottom rules, color scales, data bars, icon sets, or create new rules.

1.14 Understanding Relative, Absolute, and Mixed Cell References

When creating formulas in Excel, the way you reference cells determines how the formula will update when copied to other cells. By default, cell references are relative, meaning they will change when copied to another cell. For example, if you write "=A1" in cell B1 and then copy it to B2, the formula will adjust to "=A2". Suppose you want to keep a cell reference constant. In that case, you need to use absolute references by adding a dollar sign before the column and/or the row like this: A1.

Mixed cell references have only one of the row or column references as absolute. For example, $A1 or A$1. When copying the formula, these are useful when you want the row or column to stay the same.

1.15 Introduction to Excel Tables

Excel tables are a powerful feature that simplifies working with data ranges. To create a table, select your data range, go to the Insert tab, and click on Table. Excel tables have built-in filtering and sorting options for each column. They also have a style applied, but you can change this or remove it altogether in the Table Styles group on the Table Tools Design tab.

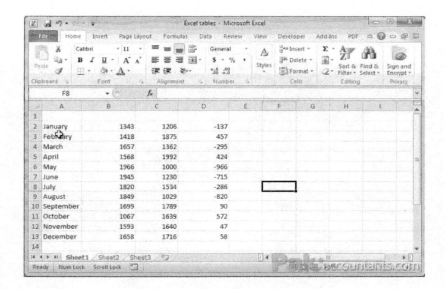

Chapter 2: User Interface of Excel 2023

The user interface (UI) of Excel 2023 is designed to help users navigate and use the application efficiently. It contains a range of tools and options that can be accessed via various components, including the ribbon, quick access toolbar, formula bar, and the status bar.

2.1 Menu Bar

The Menu Bar, located at the top of the Excel window, contains several tabs, including File, Home, Insert, Page Layout, Formulas, Data, Review, View, and Help.

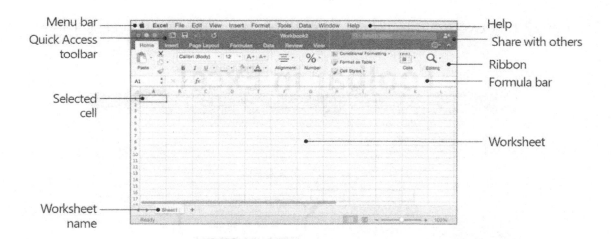

1. **File**: This tab opens the backstage view where you can access file-related commands such as New, Open, Save, Print, Options, and more.
2. **Home**: This is where you can find the most commonly used options such as cut, copy, paste, format cells, and sort & and filter.
3. **Insert**: This tab is used to insert elements like tables, pictures, charts, forms, headers & footers, etc.
4. **Page Layout**: Here you can find options to manage page setup, themes, scale to fit, sheet options, and arrange.

5. **Formulas**: This is where you can manage all the functions and formulas. It includes function library, defined names, formula auditing, and calculation.
6. **Data**: This tab has tools to connect to external data sources, sort & filter, data tools, and outline.
7. **Review**: This tab provides access to tools for spelling, accessibility, comments, and changes (like protecting and sharing the workbook).
8. **View**: This tab allows you to change workbook views, show/hide specific items, zoom, and manage windows.
9. **Help**: This tab provides access to Excel's built-in Help system, as well as links to online resources and training.

2.2 Toolbars

Excel 2023 has two main toolbars: The Ribbon and the Quick Access Toolbar.

1. **The Ribbon**: The Ribbon, located at the top of the Excel window, is where you can access almost all of Excel's commands. It's organized into tabs, and each tab is further divided into groups. For example, the Home tab has groups like Clipboard, Font, Alignment, and Number. Each group contains relevant commands.

2. **Quick Access Toolbar**: This is a customizable toolbar that contains a set of commands independent of the tab currently displayed on the Ribbon. By default, it includes the Save, Undo, and Redo commands, but you can add other commands according to your preference.

2.3 Working Area

The main working area in Excel 2023 consists of cells organized as rows and columns. Each cell is identified by a unique address made up of its column letter and row number. For example, the cell in the top left corner is cell A1, meaning column A, row 1.

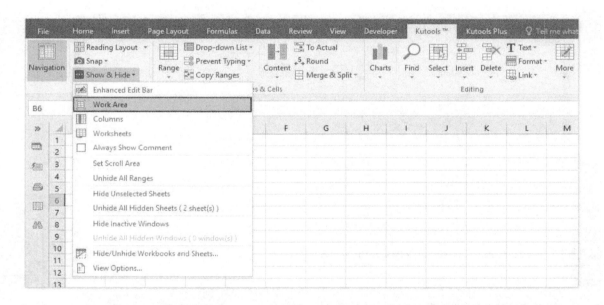

Other important elements in the working area include:

1. **Column Headers**: These are labeled with letters (A, B, C, etc.). The labeling continues with double letters after Z (AA, AB, AC, and so forth).
2. **Row Headers**: These are numbered from 1 to 1,048,576.
3. **Formula Bar**: This is where you can enter and edit data or formulas in the current cell.
4. **Sheet Tabs**: These are located at the bottom of the Excel window. By default, a new Excel workbook starts with one worksheet. You can add more by clicking the plus icon to the right of the sheet tabs.

2.5 AutoFill and Flash Fill

AutoFill and Flash Fill are essential tools to streamline data entry and are surprisingly easy to use. In Excel, you can autofill cells by selecting the cell with the initial value, then click and drag the small square at the lower right corner across the cells you want to fill. You'll see that Excel automatically fills the cells with values based on the pattern in the selected cells.

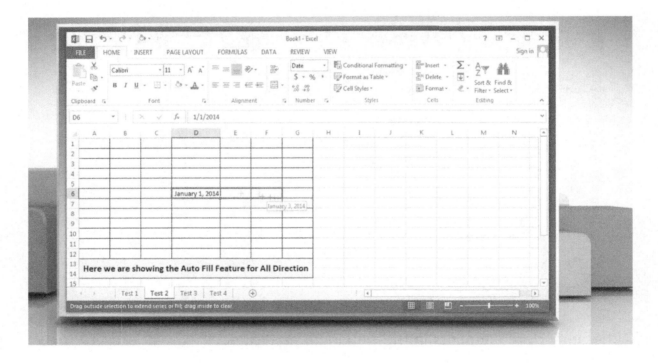

Flash Fill takes this a step further. Imagine you have a list of names in the format "First Last" and want to separate the first and last names into different columns. Instead of doing it manually, you can start typing the first few names in a new column, and Excel's Flash Fill will recognize the pattern and suggest completing the rest for you. To accept the suggestion, simply press Enter.

2.6 The Fill Series Tool

Let's say you want to generate a series of dates, from January 1 to December 31. Instead of typing each date manually, you can use the Fill Series tool. Start by typing the first date in a cell. Then select that cell, go to the Home tab, click on the Fill dropdown in the Editing group, and choose Series. In the Series dialog box, you would then select Date for Type, Day for Date Unit, and enter the end date under Stop Value.

2.7 Understanding Number Formats

In Excel, data can be represented in various formats, such as General, Number, Currency, Date, Time, Percentage, and more. Changing the number format doesn't change the underlying data, just how it's displayed. For example, if you type "1234" into a cell, Excel treats it as a number, but if you change the number format to Currency, it will display as "$1,234.00".

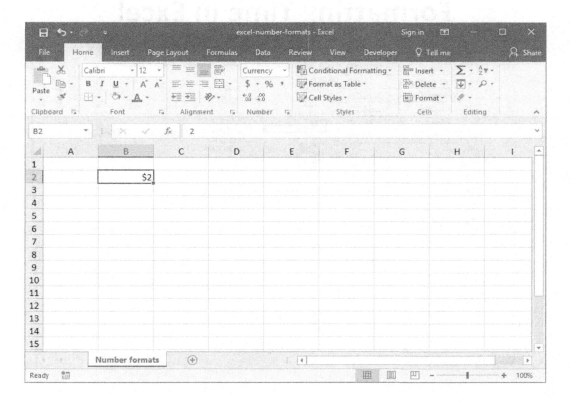

2.8 Excel's Text Functions

Excel's text functions can help you manipulate text data in various ways. For example, the LEFT function extracts a given number of characters from the start of a text string. If you have "Excel 2023" in a cell and use the formula **=LEFT(A1, 5)**, Excel will return "Excel".

2.9 Dates and Times in Excel

In Excel, dates are stored as numbers, with each day representing a whole number. January 1, 1900, is 1, and every day after that is a larger number. Times are stored as decimal numbers, representing a portion of a day. For example, 12:00 PM is 0.5, as it's half of a day. This system allows you to perform calculations with dates and times, such as subtracting one date from another to get the number of days in between.

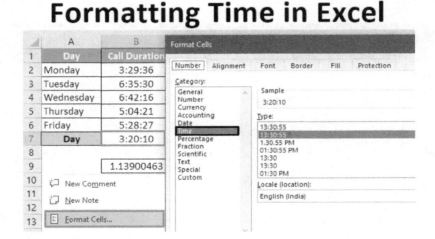

Chapter 3: Fundamental Principles of Excel

Excel is built on a few fundamental principles. Understanding these is crucial for anyone looking to become proficient in its use. This chapter will cover cells, rows, columns, worksheets, how to enter and edit data, and basic cell and text formatting.

3.1 Cells, Rows, Columns, and Worksheets

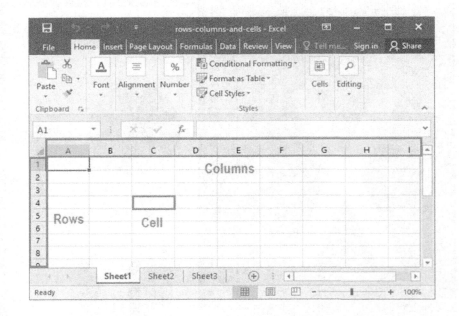

3.1.1 Cells

A cell is the basic building block of a worksheet. Each cell is defined by its unique column and row. The intersection of a column and a row is a single cell, which can contain a value, a text string, or a formula. Each cell can be identified by its cell reference, which is the column letter followed by the row number. For example, the cell in the upper-left corner of the worksheet is cell A1.

3.1.2 Rows and Columns

A row is a horizontal group of cells and a column is a vertical group of cells. Rows are identified by numbers (1, 2, 3, etc.), and columns are identified by letters (A, B, C, etc.). Excel 2023 supports 1,048,576 rows and 16,384 columns per worksheet.

3.1.3 Worksheets

A worksheet, or "sheet," is a single, two-dimensional grid of cells. Each workbook can contain multiple worksheets, and you can switch between them by clicking on their tabs at the bottom of the Excel window.

3.2 Entering and Editing Data

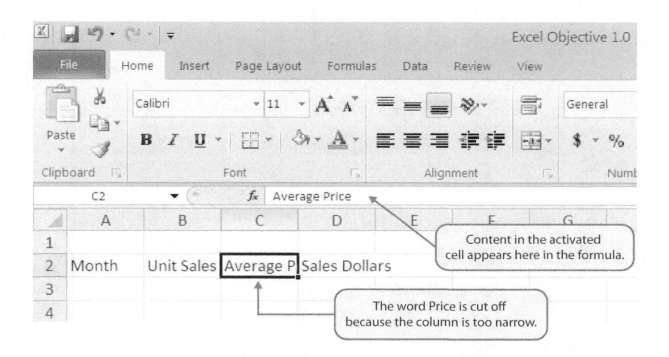

3.2.1 Entering Data

To enter data in Excel, simply select a cell and start typing. When you're done, press Enter to move down to the next cell or Tab to move to the right. If you want to enter a series of data, you can type the first few and then drag the fill handle (a small square in the bottom-right corner of the cell) to fill the rest of the series.

3.2.2 Editing Data

To edit data in a cell, you can double-click the cell and start typing or select the cell and press F2. When you're done editing, press Enter or click outside the cell to finish. You can also edit the contents of a cell in the formula bar.

3.3 Cell and Text Formatting

Excel provides a range of options to format your cells and text. You can find these options in the 'Home' tab in the ribbon.

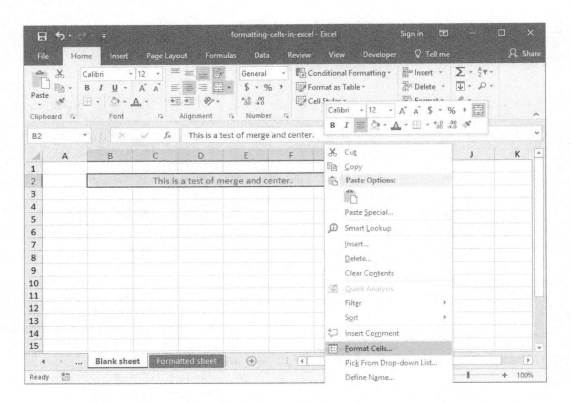

3.3.1 Cell Formatting

You can adjust the appearance of cells in many ways including fill color, font color, borders, and number formatting. Excel also allows you to adjust column width and row height, as well as align cell content vertically or horizontally.

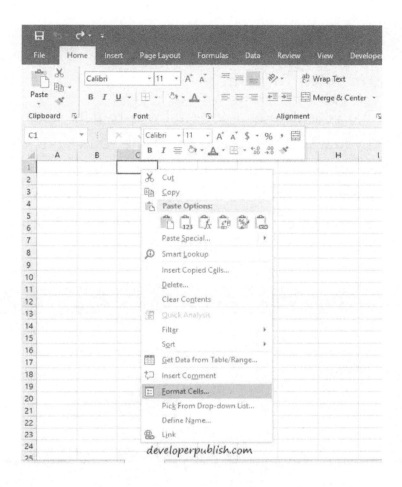

3.3.2 Text Formatting

Excel provides numerous text formatting options. You can change the font, font size, font color, and font style (bold, italic, underline, etc.). You can also apply effects like strikethrough, subscript, and superscript. Other options include text alignment, text control, and text direction.

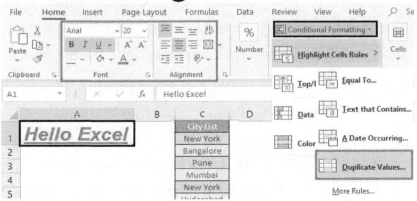

3.5 Sorting and Filtering Data

Sorting and filtering your data is a powerful way to gain insights. To sort data, select the column you want to sort, and under the "Data" tab, choose "Sort A to Z" or "Sort Z to A". You can add multiple levels of sorting by clicking on "Sort Custom". For example, if you have a spreadsheet of a store's sales data, you could sort by the item category first, then by the individual item within each category.

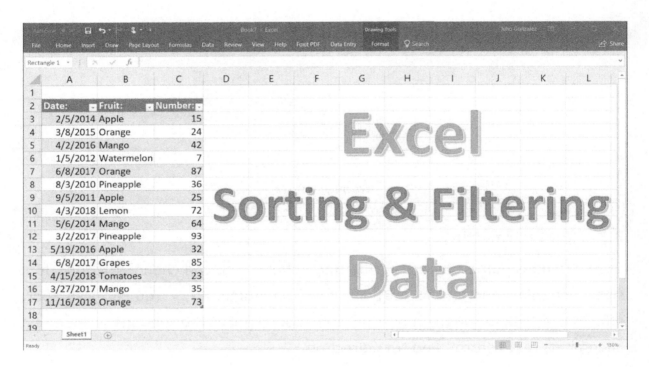

Filtering hides data that you don't need to see. To filter data, select the column you want to filter, go to the "Data" tab, and click "Filter". This will add a dropdown to the column header. When you click on the dropdown, you'll see all the unique values in the column. You can select the ones you want to see and deselect the ones you don't.

3.6 Data Validation

Data validation is a tool that helps control what data gets entered into your spreadsheet. To use it, select the cells to which you want to apply the validation, go to the "Data" tab, and click "Data Validation". For example, if you want to limit entries in a cell to whole numbers between 1 and 100, under the "Settings" tab, select "Whole number" from the "Allow" dropdown, and "between" from the "Data" dropdown, then enter 1 and 100 in the "Minimum" and "Maximum" fields.

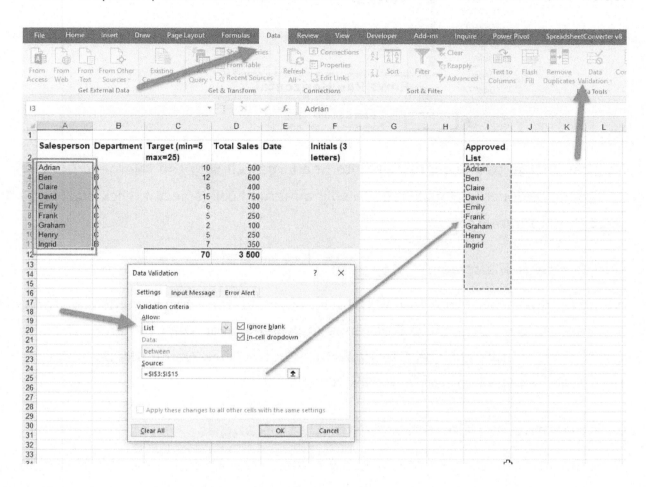

3.7 Working with Rows, Columns, and Cells

To insert a row, select a row, right-click, and choose "Insert". To delete a row, select it, right-click, and choose "Delete". You can adjust the height of a row by selecting it and dragging the bottom border of the row header. Similarly, you can insert or delete columns, and adjust their width.

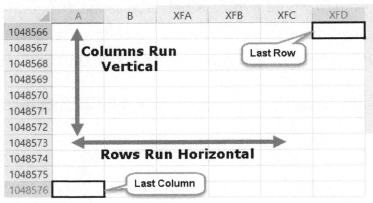

You can merge two or more cells into one large cell with the "Merge & Center" command under the "Home" tab. To split a merged cell, select it, click on "Merge & Center" to unmerge.

3.8 Named Ranges

Named ranges make your formulas easier to understand and manage. To create a named range, select the cell or range of cells that you want to name. Then, in the "Formulas" tab, click on "Define Name". In the "New Name" dialog box, type the name you want to use, and click "OK".

3.9 Formatting Cells Based on Date Ranges

Conditional formatting can be used to format cells containing dates in certain ranges. Under the "Home" tab, click on "Conditional Formatting", then "New Rule". In the "New Formatting Rule" dialog box, select "Format cells that contain", then in the "Format only cells with" section, set the condition to format the dates as desired.

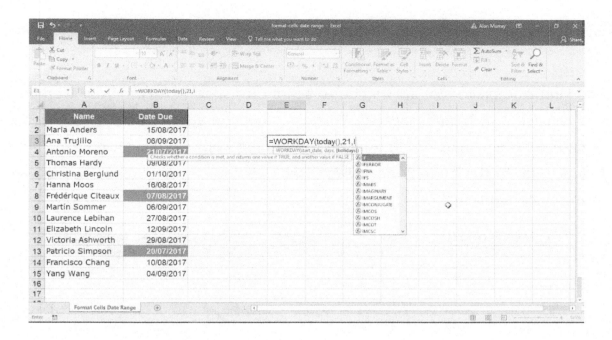

3.10 The Fill Handle

The Fill Handle is a powerful tool in Excel. It appears as a small square in the bottom-right corner of the selected cell. By clicking and dragging the Fill Handle, you can quickly copy the content of the selected cell to adjacent cells or fill them with a series of numbers, dates, or other patterns.

For instance, if you type '1' in a cell and then drag the Fill Handle down, Excel will fill the selected cells with a series of numbers (1, 2, 3, 4, etc.). If you select two cells that contain '1' and '2' respectively, and then drag the Fill Handle down, Excel will extend the series by adding 1 to the last number (1, 2, 3, 4, etc.).

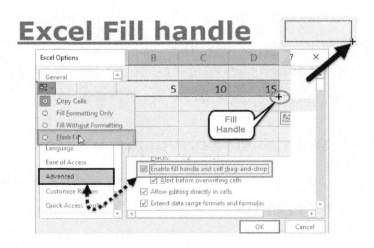

3.11 Using Find & Replace

The Find & Replace tool allows you to search for specific text in your workbook and replace it with different text. This can save you a lot of time if you need to update specific pieces of information throughout your workbook. To use Find & Replace, go to the 'Home' tab, select 'Find & Select' in the 'Editing' group, and then select 'Replace'.

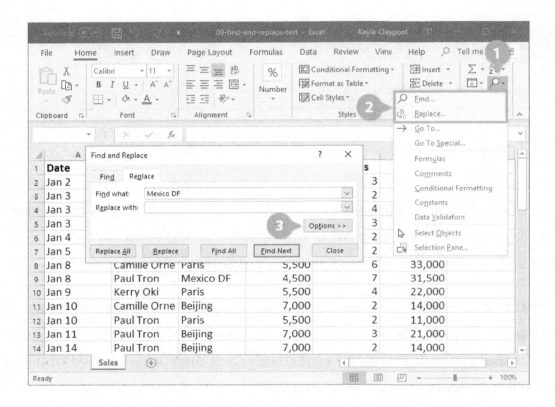

In the 'Find what:' box, type the text you're looking for. In the 'Replace with:' box, type the text you want to use instead. Click 'Find Next' to find the first instance of the text, and then click 'Replace' to replace it. If you want to replace all instances at once, click 'Replace All'.

3.12 Introduction to Basic Formulas

Excel uses formulas to perform calculations on the data in your workbook. All Excel formulas begin with an equal sign (=). For instance, you could use the formula **=A1+A2** to add the values in cells A1 and A2. Excel calculates the result of the formula and displays it in the cell where you entered the formula.

Chapter 4: Working with Data in Excel

Managing and manipulating data is at the core of what makes Excel such a powerful tool. In this chapter, we'll cover the different data types you can use, how to insert and edit data, and how to use the Find and Replace feature.

4.1 Data Types in Excel

Excel can handle a variety of data types. The most common are:

1. **Text (also known as labels or strings):** This is any combination of characters, including letters, numbers, spaces, and punctuation.
2. **Numbers**: These can be integers or decimals. They can be used in calculations, unlike text.
3. **Dates and times**: Excel can recognize a wide range of date and time formats, and it allows you to perform calculations with them.
4. **Boolean values**: These are logical values and can be TRUE or FALSE.
5. **Error-values**: These appear when there's something wrong with a formula.
6. **New Data Types in Excel 2023**: Excel 2023 introduces new data types, such as Stocks and Geography, that can pull in rich information from the internet.

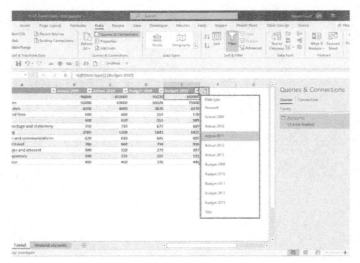

4.2 Inserting and Editing Data

4.2.1 Inserting Data

To insert data in a cell, simply select the cell and start typing. You can navigate between cells using the arrow keys, and you can move to the next row by pressing Enter. Excel also allows you to fill cells automatically with the fill handle and the auto-fill feature.

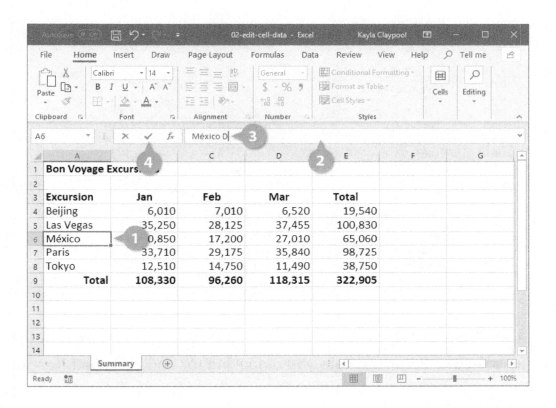

4.2.2 Editing Data

To edit data in a cell, you can double-click the cell or select it and press F2. You can also edit cell contents in the formula bar. To delete data, select the cell and press Delete.

4.3 Find and Replace Data

The Find and Replace feature in Excel can help you locate specific information in your workbook. You can also use it to automatically replace data.

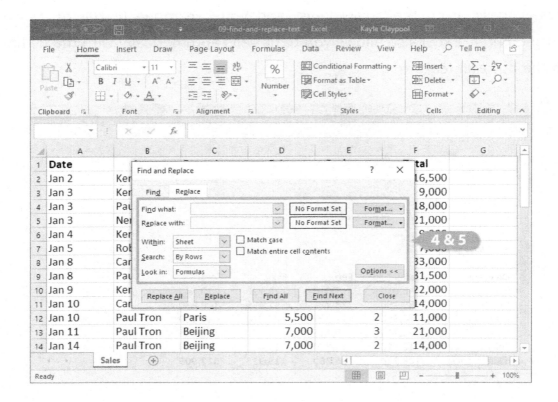

1. **Find**: Press Ctrl+F to open the Find and Replace dialog box with the Find tab selected. Enter the data you're looking for and click Find Next or Find All.
2. **Replace**: Press Ctrl+H to open the Find and Replace dialog box with the Replace tab selected. Enter the data you want to replace and the data you want to replace it with, then click Replace or Replace All.

4.4 Sorting and Filtering Data

Sorting and filtering data are two essential tasks in Excel that allow you to organize and analyze data more effectively.

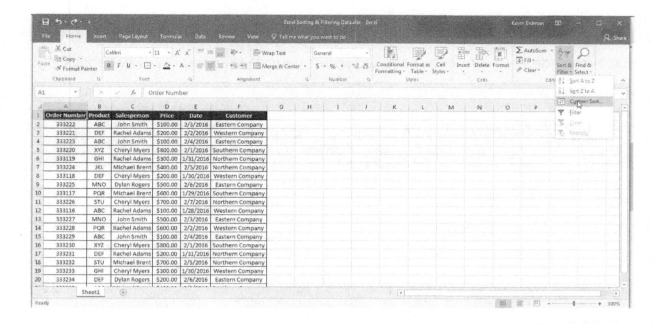

4.4.1 Sorting Data

Sorting can help you arrange your data in a meaningful order (e.g., from smallest to largest, A to Z, or by color or icon). Here's how to sort data:

1. **Single Column Sort**: Select any cell within the column you want to sort, go to the 'Home' tab > 'Editing' group > 'Sort & Filter'. Choose either 'Sort A to Z' or 'Sort Z to A' as needed.

2. **Multi-column Sort**: If you want to sort by more than one column, select your data, go to the 'Data' tab > 'Sort & Filter' group > 'Sort'. In the dialog box, add the levels of sorting.

4.4.2 Filtering Data

Filtering can help you display only the data that meets certain criteria. Here's how to filter data:

1. Select any cell within your data range, go to the 'Home' tab > 'Editing' group > 'Sort & Filter' > 'Filter'. This will add drop-down arrows to each column header.

2. Click the drop-down arrow for the column you want to filter. Check or uncheck the boxes to set your filter, and then click 'OK'.

4.5 Formatting Data

Excel provides numerous options to format your data to improve readability and emphasis.

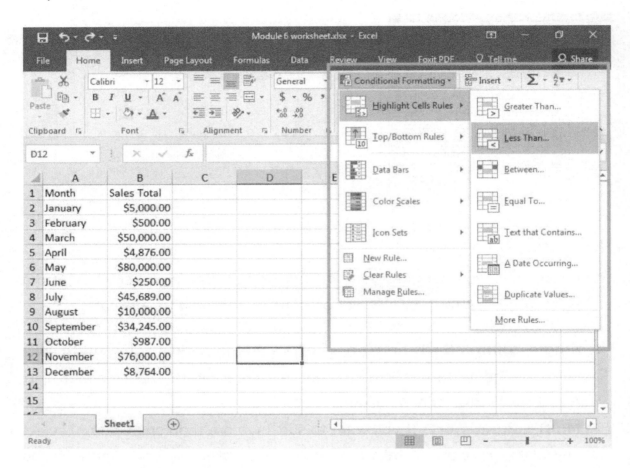

4.5.1 Conditional Formatting

Conditional formatting allows you to set rules for cell formatting based on the cell's value. For example, you can highlight cells that contain values above a certain threshold:

1. Select the cells you want to format.
2. Go to the 'Home' tab > 'Styles' group > 'Conditional Formatting'.
3. Select the type of rule you want to apply and set the criteria.

4.5.2 Cell Styles and Themes

Excel provides predefined cell styles and themes that you can apply to your data for a professional and cohesive look:

1. To apply a cell style, select your cells, go to the 'Home' tab > 'Styles' group > 'Cell Styles', and select the style you want to apply.
2. To apply a theme, go to the 'Page Layout' tab > 'Themes' group > 'Themes', and select the theme you want to apply.

4.6 Working with Sheets

Excel workbooks are composed of multiple sheets, and managing them effectively can greatly improve your workflow. To insert a new sheet, click on the '+' button at the bottom of Excel. To rename a sheet, right-click the sheet's tab, select 'Rename', and type the new name. You can also color code your tabs by right-clicking them and selecting 'Tab Color'. To move a sheet, click and drag the tab to its new location. If you want to copy a sheet, right-click the tab, select 'Move or Copy', choose where to place the copy, and make sure the 'Create a copy' box is checked.

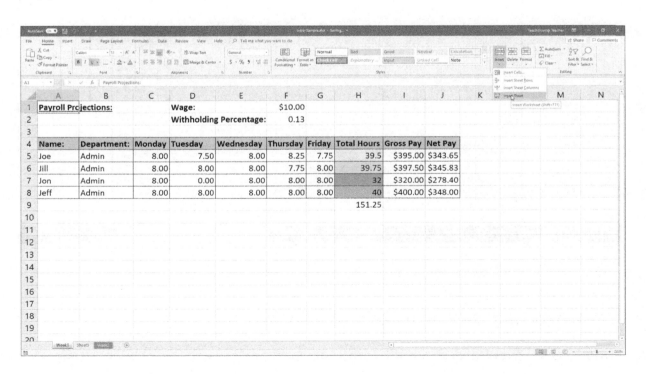

4.7 Cell References and Cell Addressing

In Excel, each cell is identified by a unique cell address composed of the column letter and row number (like 'A1'). If you use this address in a formula, it's a relative cell reference, meaning it will change if you copy the formula to a different cell. However, if you want the cell reference to stay constant, you can make it absolute by adding a $ before the column letter and row number (like 'A1'). This won't change even if you copy the formula elsewhere.

4.8 Basic Math Operations

Excel supports all the basic math operations. For example, to add two numbers, you could use a formula like '=A1+B1', where A1 and B1 are the cell addresses of the numbers you want to add. Similarly, you can subtract ('-'), multiply ('*'), and divide ('/').

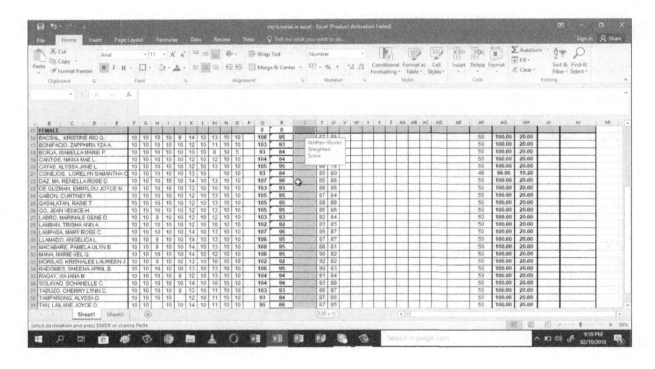

4.9 Introduction to Functions

Functions in Excel are pre-built formulas that perform specific calculations. For instance, the SUM function adds up all the numbers in a range of cells. To use it, you would type '=SUM(A1:B1)', where 'A1:B1' is the range of cells you want to add up. Excel has hundreds of functions, each with a specific purpose.

4.10 Introduction to Formulas

A formula in Excel is a way to perform calculations on the values in your worksheet. It always starts with an equals sign ('='). After the equals sign, you can include numbers, cell references, operators (like '+'), and functions. When you press Enter, Excel calculates the result of the formula and displays the result in the cell.

Excursion	Jan	Feb	Mar	Total
Beijing	6,010	7,010	6,520	19,540
Las Vegas	35,250	28,125	37,455	100,830
Mexico City	20,850	17,200	27,010	65,060
Paris	33,710	29,175	35,840	98,725
Tokyo	12,510	14,750	11,490	38,750
Total	108,330	96,260	118,315	322,905

Chapter 5: Formulas and Functions in Excel

One of Excel's most powerful features is its ability to calculate mathematical information in your worksheets. In this chapter, we'll look at how to create basic formulas, use some common functions, and manage named ranges.

5.1 Creating Basic Formulas

Every formula in Excel starts with an equal sign (=). This is followed by the elements to be calculated (the operands), which are separated by calculation operators. For example, to add two numbers, the formula would be **=A1+B1**, assuming those two numbers are located in cells A1 and B1.

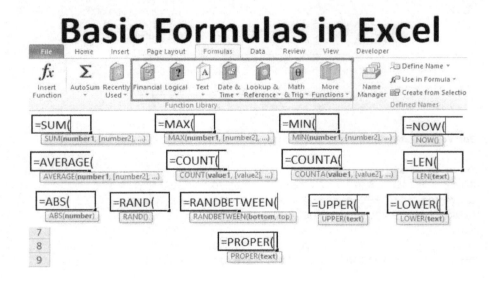

Excel follows the standard mathematical order of operations. If you want to change the order of operations, you can use parentheses. For example, in the formula **=A1+B1*C1**, Excel calculates the multiplication before the addition. If you want it to add first, the formula would be **=(A1+B1)*C1**.

5.2 Using Functions

Excel includes many common functions, which can be used to quickly calculate sums, averages, counts, maximums, minimums, and so on.

1. **SUM**: **=SUM(A1:A10)** adds all the numbers in cells A1 through A10.
2. **AVERAGE**: **=AVERAGE(A1:A10)** calculates the average of the numbers in cells A1 through A10.
3. **COUNT**: **=COUNT(A1:A10)** counts the number of cells that contain numbers in the range A1 through A10.
4. **MAX**: **=MAX(A1:A10)** returns the largest number in the range A1 through A10.
5. **MIN**: **=MIN(A1:A10)** returns the smallest number in the range A1 through A10.

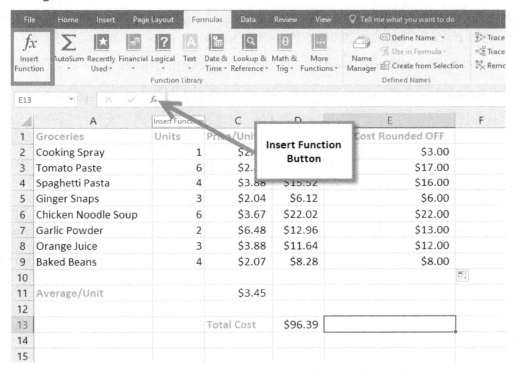

In addition to these basic functions, Excel also provides a wide range of more advanced functions that can be used for financial, logical, text, date and time, lookup and reference, math and trigonometry, and statistical operations.

5.3 Managing Named Ranges

Named ranges are a useful feature in Excel that allows you to assign a meaningful name to a cell or range of cells. This can make your formulas much easier to read and write.

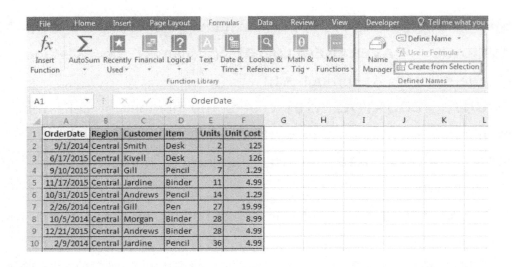

To create a named range, select the cell(s) you want to name, then go to the 'Formulas' tab > 'Defined Names' group > 'Define Name'. In the 'New Name' dialog box, type the name you want to use, and click 'OK'.

Once a named range is created, you can use it in your formulas. For example, if you have a named range "sales" for cells A1:A10, you can calculate the sum of those cells using **=SUM(sales)**.

Remember to always review your formulas and functions for accuracy, and take advantage of Excel's formula auditing tools to troubleshoot and correct any errors.

5.4 Advanced Functions

Excel is equipped with a multitude of advanced functions that cater to different types of data manipulation and calculation. Some of these include:

5.4.1 Logical Functions

Logical functions return values based on complex or multiple test conditions. Some frequently used logical functions are IF, AND, OR, NOT, XOR.

For example, **=IF(A1>10, "Pass", "Fail")** checks whether the value in cell A1 is greater than 10. If it is, it returns "Pass"; if it's not, it returns "Fail".

5.4.2 Lookup Functions

Lookup functions are used to find specific data in your spreadsheet. The two main lookup functions are VLOOKUP and HLOOKUP. In Excel 2023, XLOOKUP function is introduced which overcomes many limitations of VLOOKUP and HLOOKUP.

For example, **=VLOOKUP(B2, A1:C10, 2, FALSE)** will look for the value in cell B2 in the first column of the range A1:C10, and it will return the value in the same row from the second column of the range.

5.4.3 Text Functions

Text functions can be used to manipulate strings in Excel. Some frequently used text functions are LEFT, RIGHT, MID, TRIM, UPPER, LOWER, PROPER, CONCATENATE (or CONCAT in Excel 2023), and TEXTJOIN.

For example, **=UPPER(A1)** will convert the text in cell A1 to upper case.

5.5 Array Formulas

An array formula is a formula that can perform multiple calculations on one or more items within an array. Array formulas are enclosed between braces **{ }** and are entered by pressing Ctrl+Shift+Enter.

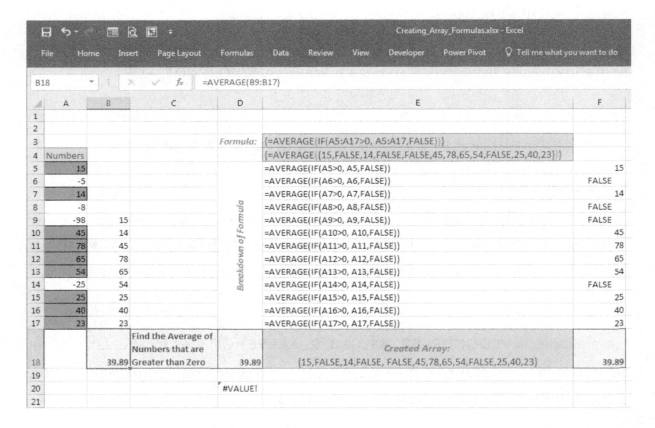

For example, **=MAX(A1:A10-B1:B10)** entered as an array formula will return the largest value of the subtraction of corresponding values in the ranges A1:A10 and B1:B10.

5.6 Error Handling in Excel

Understanding and rectifying errors is crucial when working with Excel formulas. Common errors include #DIV/0!, #NAME?, #N/A, #NULL!, #NUM!, #REF!, and #VALUE!. Each error type signifies a different issue with your formula or the data the formula is referencing.

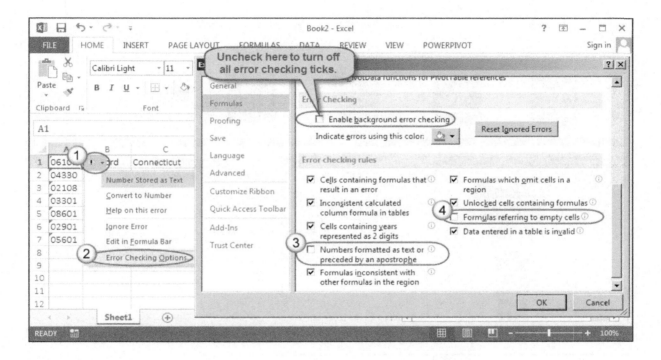

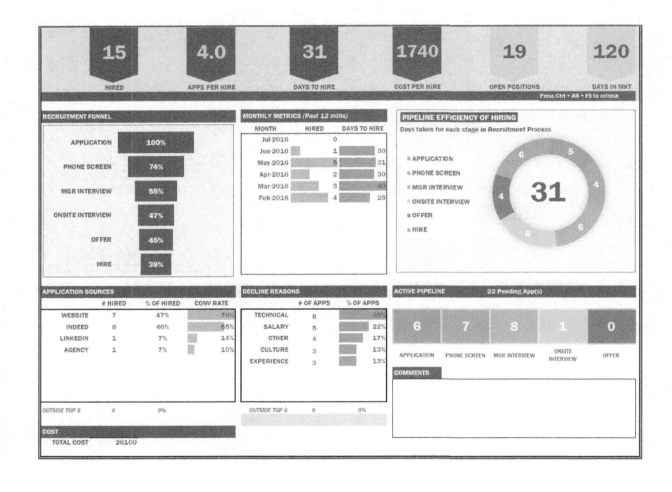

15	4.0	31	1740	19	120
HIRED	APPS PER HIRE	DAYS TO HIRE	COST PER HIRE	OPEN POSITIONS	DAYS IN MKT

Press Ctrl + Alt + F5 to refresh

RECRUITMENT FUNNEL

Stage	%
APPLICATION	100%
PHONE SCREEN	74%
MGR INTERVIEW	55%
ONSITE INTERVIEW	47%
OFFER	45%
HIRE	39%

MONTHLY METRICS (Past 12 mths)

MONTH	HIRED	DAYS TO HIRE
Jul-2016	0	
Jun-2016	1	30
May-2016	5	31
Apr-2016	2	30
Mar-2016	3	40
Feb-2016	4	26

PIPELINE EFFICIENCY OF HIRING

Days taken for each stage in Recruitment Process

- APPLICATION
- PHONE SCREEN
- MGR INTERVIEW
- ONSITE INTERVIEW
- OFFER
- HIRE

31

6 5
4
4
6
6

APPLICATION SOURCES

	# HIRED	% OF HIRED	CONV RATE
WEBSITE	7	47%	70%
INDEED	6	40%	55%
LINKEDIN	1	7%	14%
AGENCY	1	7%	10%
OUTSIDE TOP 8	0	0%	

DECLINE REASONS

	# OF APPS	% OF APPS
TECHNICAL	8	35%
SALARY	5	22%
OTHER	4	17%
CULTURE	3	13%
EXPERIENCE	3	13%
OUTSIDE TOP 8	0	0%

ACTIVE PIPELINE   22 Pending App(s)

6	7	8	1	0
APPLICATION	PHONE SCREEN	MGR INTERVIEW	ONSITE INTERVIEW	OFFER

COMMENTS

COST

TOTAL COST	26100

Chapter 6: Working with PivotTables and PivotCharts

PivotTables and PivotCharts are powerful features in Excel that allow you to analyze large amounts of data quickly and easily. In this chapter, we'll look at how to create and modify PivotTables and PivotCharts, and how to use slicers and timelines for filtering.

6.1 Creating a PivotTable

PivotTables can summarize large amounts of data by grouping it into categories and providing summarized calculations.

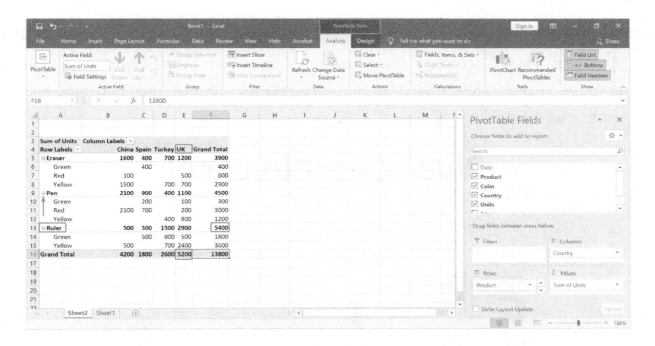

To create a PivotTable:

1. Organize your data in columns with headers. Make sure your dataset has no blank rows or columns.
2. Click anywhere in your dataset, then go to the 'Insert' tab > 'Tables' group > 'PivotTable'. In the 'Create PivotTable' dialog box, ensure the correct data range is selected, choose where you want to place your PivotTable, and click 'OK'.

3. In the PivotTable Field List pane, drag the fields to the appropriate area (Filters, Columns, Rows, or Values). Excel will automatically update the PivotTable.

6.2 Modifying a PivotTable

You can modify a PivotTable by adding or removing fields or changing the calculation type (e.g., sum, average, count, max, min). You can also sort and filter the PivotTable data, format the PivotTable for better readability, and create calculated fields or items.

6.3 Creating a PivotChart

PivotCharts complement PivotTables by providing visual representations of the PivotTable data. To create a PivotChart, click anywhere in the PivotTable, then go to the 'Insert' tab > 'Charts' group > 'PivotChart'. Choose the chart type you want to use and click 'OK'.

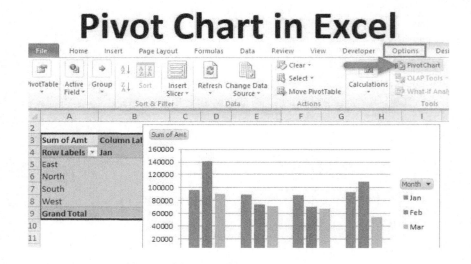

6.4 Using Slicers and Timelines

Slicers and Timelines provide simple, intuitive ways to filter PivotTable data.

1. **Slicers**: To insert a slicer, click anywhere in the PivotTable, then go to the 'PivotTable Tools: Analyze' tab > 'Filter' group > 'Insert Slicer'. Select the

fields you want to create slicers for and click 'OK'. You can select items from the slicer to filter the PivotTable.

2. **Timelines**: Timelines are a type of slicer that works with date fields. To insert a timeline, click anywhere in the PivotTable, then go to the 'PivotTable Tools: Analyze' tab > 'Filter' group > 'Insert Timeline'. Select the date field you want to create a timeline for and click 'OK'. You can select time periods from the timeline to filter the PivotTable.

With a proper understanding and usage of PivotTables and PivotCharts, you can dramatically enhance your data analysis capabilities in Excel.

6.5 Advanced PivotTable Techniques

PivotTables offer a variety of advanced techniques that can be used to enhance your data analysis.

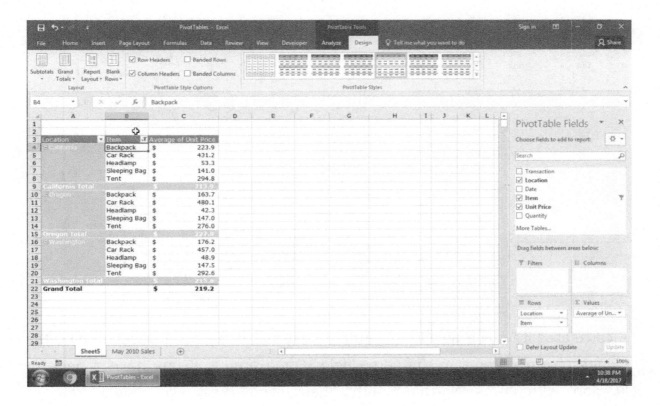

6.5.1 Using Calculated Fields and Items

Calculated fields and items allow you to add additional data to your PivotTable that is derived from the existing fields.

A calculated field is a new field that performs a calculation on the values of another field. For example, if you have a field for 'Quantity' and a field for 'Price', you could create a calculated field for 'Total Sales' (=Quantity*Price).

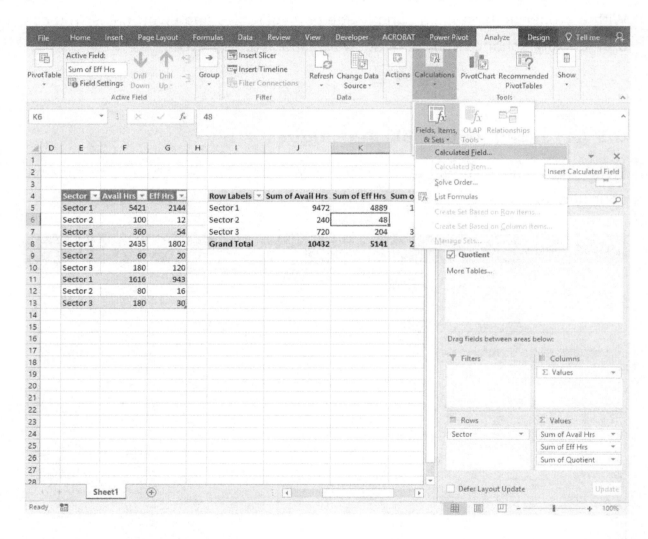

A calculated item is a new item within a field that performs a calculation on the values of other items in the same field. For example, if you have a field for 'Region' with items 'North', 'South', 'East', and 'West', you could create a calculated item for 'North+South'.

6.5.2 Using the GETPIVOTDATA Function

The GETPIVOTDATA function can be used to retrieve specific data from a PivotTable. The syntax is **=GETPIVOTDATA(data_field, pivot_table, [field1, item1, field2, item2], ...)**. The data_field is the name of the field you want to retrieve data from, and the pivot_table is the cell reference of any cell in the PivotTable. The field and item pairs are optional, and you can use as many pairs as you need to define the specific data you want to retrieve.

6.5.3 Creating a PivotTable from Multiple Ranges

If your data is spread across multiple ranges, you can use the 'Data Model' feature to create a PivotTable that includes all the data. When creating the PivotTable, in the 'Create PivotTable' dialog box, check the 'Add this data to the Data Model' box. You can then use the 'All' tab in the PivotTable Field List to add fields from any of the ranges to the PivotTable.

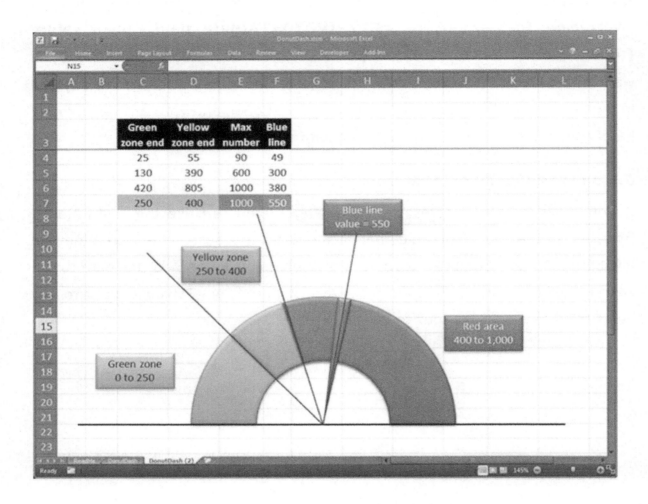

Chapter 7: Data Visualization with Charts and Graphs

Visual representation of data is a fundamental part of data analysis. In this chapter, we'll explore how to create and customize various types of charts and graphs in Excel to effectively visualize your data.

7.1 Creating Basic Charts

Excel offers a variety of charts that you can use depending on the nature of your data. The common types of charts include Column, Line, Pie, Bar, Area, and Scatter.

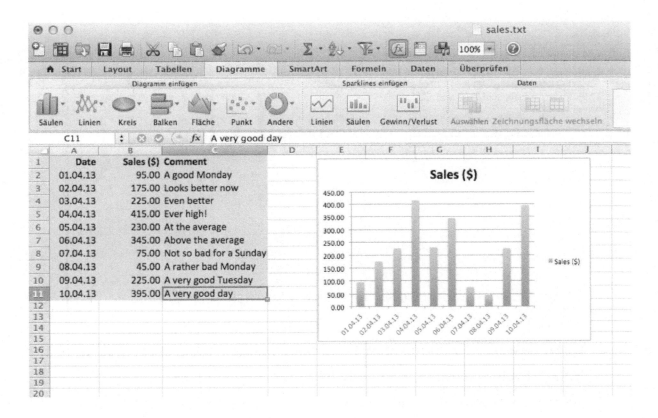

1. Select the data that you want to represent as a chart.
2. Go to the 'Insert' tab > 'Charts' group.
3. Select the chart type you want to use. Excel will automatically create the chart for you.

7.2 Customizing Charts

Once a chart is created, you can customize it in many ways to enhance its readability and visual appeal:

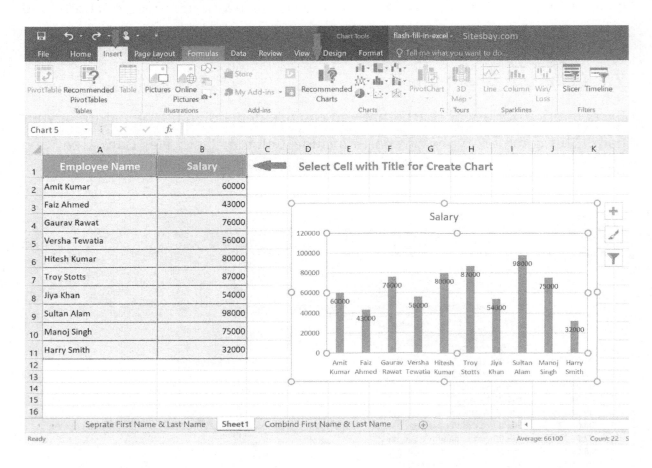

1. **Chart Title**: To add or edit the chart title, click on the chart and go to the 'Chart Tools: Layout' tab > 'Labels' group > 'Chart Title'.

2. **Data Labels**: To add or edit data labels, click on the chart and go to the 'Chart Tools: Layout' tab > 'Labels' group > 'Data Labels'.

3. **Axes**: To modify the axes, click on the chart and go to the 'Chart Tools: Layout' tab > 'Axes' group.

4. **Legend**: To modify the legend, click on the chart and go to the 'Chart Tools: Layout' tab > 'Labels' group > 'Legend'.

5. **Chart Style**: To change the chart style, click on the chart and go to the 'Chart Tools: Design' tab > 'Chart Styles' group.

7.3 Advanced Chart Types

In addition to the basic chart types, Excel also offers some advanced chart types:

1. **Combo Chart**: Combo charts can display multiple chart types (like column and line) in a single chart. This is useful when the data that you want to plot has different types or scales.
2. **Histogram**: A Histogram shows the frequency of data within certain intervals.
3. **Pareto Chart**: A Pareto chart is a type of chart that contains both bars and a line graph, where individual values are represented in descending order by bars, and the cumulative total is represented by the line.
4. **Waterfall Chart**: A waterfall chart shows a running total as values are added or subtracted. It's useful for understanding how an initial value is affected by a series of positive and negative changes.

7.4 Using Sparklines

Sparklines are mini charts placed in single cells, each representing a row of data in your selection. They provide a quick way to see trends at a glance.

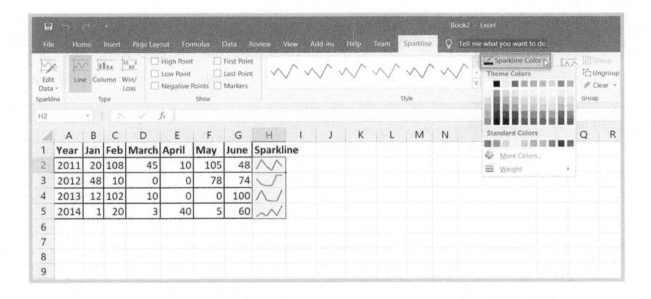

To create a sparkline, select the cell where you want the sparkline to appear, go to the 'Insert' tab > 'Sparklines' group, and choose the sparkline type you want to use.

7.5 Advanced Chart Customization Techniques

For a more comprehensive data analysis, Excel offers several advanced chart customization techniques:

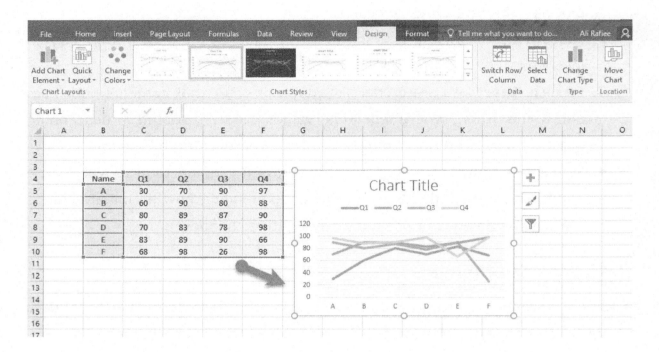

7.5.1 Adding Trendlines to Charts

A trendline, or line of best fit, can be added to scatter plot, line, column, and bar charts. Trendlines show trends or tendencies in your data, help to reveal patterns, and can forecast future data points.

To add a trendline, click on the data series and then go to the 'Chart Tools: Design' tab > 'Chart Layouts' group > 'Add Chart Element' > 'Trendline'.

7.5.2 Adding Secondary Axes

When your chart has two data series that have different scales, you can add a secondary vertical axis on the right side of the chart.

To add a secondary axis, click on the data series and then go to the 'Chart Tools: Format' tab > 'Current Selection' group > 'Format Selection'. In the 'Format Data Series' pane, under 'Series Options', check the 'Secondary Axis' box.

7.5.3 Creating Dynamic Charts

Dynamic charts automatically update to reflect changes in the source data. This can be achieved by using Excel tables as the source data for your charts. When you add or remove data from your Excel table, the chart will automatically update to reflect the changes.

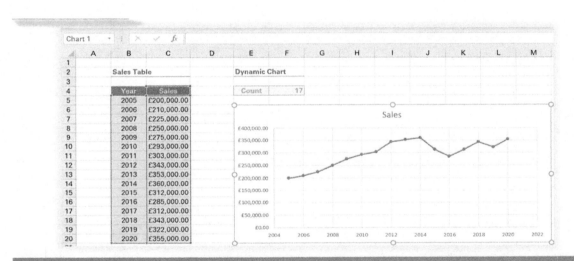

7.5.4 Using Chart Templates

If you've customized a chart and want to use the same formatting and design for other charts, you can save it as a template and apply it to new charts.

To save a chart as a template, click on the chart, then go to the 'Chart Tools: Design' tab > 'Type' group > 'Save as Template'. To use a chart template, when creating a new chart, go to the 'Insert' tab > 'Charts' group > 'All Charts' > 'Templates', and select the template you want to use.

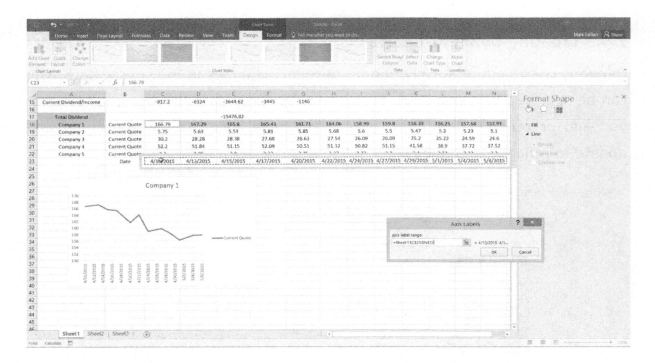

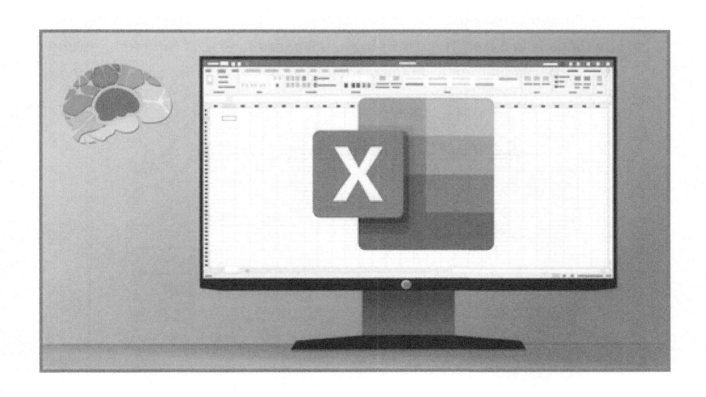

Chapter 8: Mastering Excel Functions and Formulas

Excel provides a large library of functions and formulas to perform a wide range of calculations and operations. This chapter will discuss some of the most commonly used functions and demonstrate how to construct and edit formulas.

8.1 Advanced Formulas and Functions

In addition to basic functions like SUM, Excel has more complex functions that can perform advanced calculations. Functions like VLOOKUP, INDEX, MATCH, and IF statements allow users to make complex decisions, manipulate data, and perform lookups in Excel. The use of these advanced functions can often replace the need for manual data manipulation, saving you time and improving accuracy.

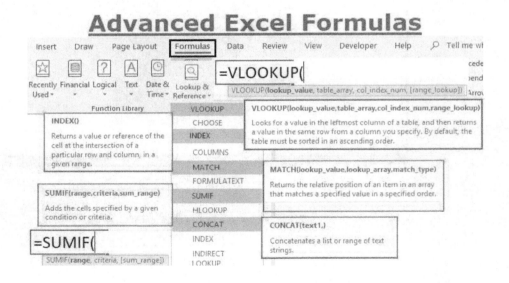

For instance, the VLOOKUP function can be used to find a corresponding value in a table based on a lookup value. If you have a table of employee names and their IDs, and you want to find the ID of a specific employee, you can use VLOOKUP. The formula would look something like this: **=VLOOKUP("EmployeeName", A2:B100, 2, FALSE)**, where "EmployeeName" is the name of the employee you're looking for, A2:B100 is the range of the table, 2 indicates that the IDs are in the second column of the range, and FALSE specifies that you want an exact match.

8.2 Array Formulas

Array formulas allow you to perform operations that involve multiple ranges or arrays of data rather than single data points. An example of an array formula could be **{=MAX(A2:A10-B2:B10)}**, which subtracts each value in the range B2:B10 from the corresponding value in A2:A10 and returns the maximum difference.

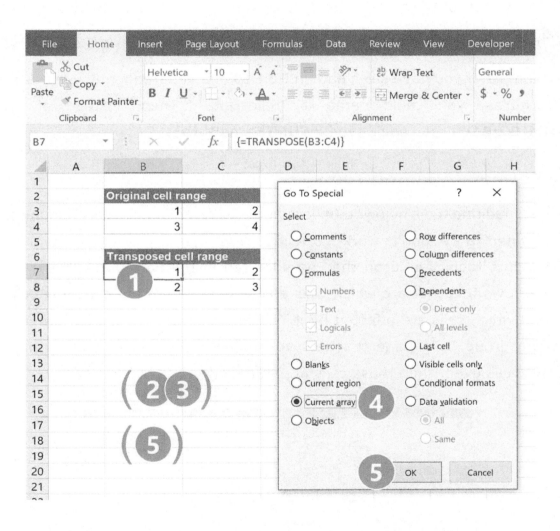

To enter an array formula, you type the formula in a cell then press Ctrl+Shift+Enter, rather than just Enter. If you do this correctly, Excel will display the formula enclosed in curly braces {}.

8.3 Named Ranges

Named ranges are a useful feature in Excel that allows you to assign a name to a cell or range of cells. This can make formulas easier to read and write. To create a named range, you select the cell(s) you want to name, click in the Name Box (to the left of the formula bar), type the name you want to use, and press Enter.

For example, if you have sales data in B2:B10 and you frequently use this range in formulas, you could name it "SalesData". Then, instead of typing **=SUM(B2:B10)**, you could type **=SUM(SalesData)**.

8.4 Formula Auditing Tools

Formula auditing tools help you understand how formulas work and troubleshoot them when they don't work correctly. The Trace Precedents and Trace Dependents tools, found on the Formulas tab in the Formula Auditing group, show arrows that indicate which cells affect the value of the currently selected cell and which cells are affected by it. The Watch Window, also in the Formula Auditing group, is a pane that lets you monitor the values and formulas in specific cells even when those cells aren't in view.

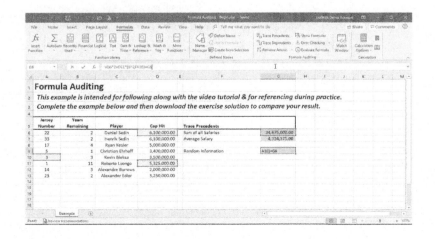

8.5 Understanding and Fixing Formula Errors

Excel provides several types of error messages, like **#VALUE!**, **#REF!**, and **#DIV/0!**, to help you understand and fix problems with your formulas. Each error type indicates a different kind of problem. For example, **#VALUE!** means that a formula is trying to perform an operation on a cell that contains non-numeric data, while **#REF!** means that a formula refers to a cell that doesn't exist (often because it was deleted).

8.6 Understanding Array Formulas

Array formulas allow you to perform complex calculations that can't be done with regular formulas. They are used to perform multiple calculations on one or more items in an array, and return either a single result or multiple results.

There are two types of array formulas: those that return a single result (like **=SUM(A1:A10*B1:B10)**) and those that return multiple results (like **{=A1:A10*B1:B10}** which multiplies each corresponding element in two arrays).

To enter an array formula, type the formula in the cell, and then press Ctrl+Shift+Enter instead of just Enter. Excel wraps the formula in curly braces **{}** to indicate it's an array formula.

8.7 Error Handling in Excel Formulas

Excel provides several tools and functions to help with error handling in formulas.

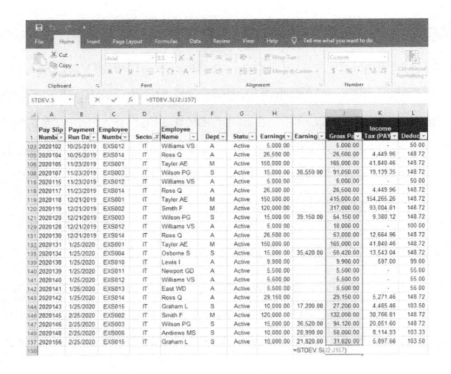

1. **IFERROR Function**: This function returns a value you specify if a formula evaluates to an error; otherwise, it returns the result of the formula. The syntax is **=IFERROR(value, value_if_error)**.

2. **ERROR.TYPE Function**: This function returns a number that corresponds to the error value. The syntax is **=ERROR.TYPE(error_val)**.

3. **Error Checking Tool**: The Error Checking tool (under 'Formulas' tab > 'Formula Auditing' group > 'Error Checking') can be used to check for common errors in formulas.

8.8 Using Named Ranges in Formulas

Named ranges can make formulas easier to read and understand. Instead of using cell references like A1 or B2:B10, you can use a descriptive name like "Sales" or "Cost". To define a named range, select the cells you want to include, and then go to 'Formulas' tab > 'Defined Names' group > 'Define Name'.

EXCEL

MULTIPLE

WORKSHEETS

Chapter 9: Working with Multiple Worksheets and Workbooks

Excel allows you to work with multiple worksheets and workbooks simultaneously. This chapter will explore the different ways of organizing, navigating, and calculating data across multiple worksheets and workbooks.

9.1 Organizing Worksheets

In Excel, you can easily add, delete, move, or copy worksheets. The options for these operations can be found by right-clicking on a worksheet tab or going to the 'Home' tab > 'Cells' group > 'Format' > 'Organize Sheets'.

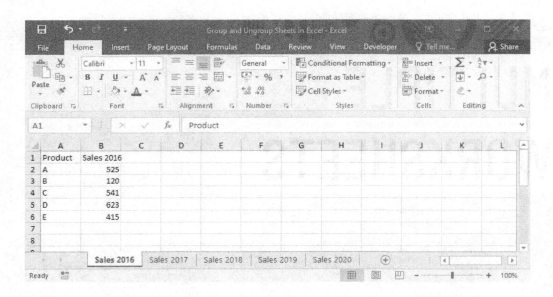

You can also rename a worksheet by double-clicking on the worksheet tab and typing the new name.

9.2 Navigating Between Worksheets

You can navigate between worksheets by clicking on the worksheet tabs at the bottom of the Excel window. You can also use the keyboard shortcuts Ctrl+PgDn to go to the next worksheet and Ctrl+PgUp to go to the previous worksheet.

9.3 Referencing Cells in Other Worksheets

You can reference cells in other worksheets by using a formula that includes the worksheet name followed by an exclamation mark and the cell reference. For example, **=Sheet2!A1** refers to cell A1 in Sheet2.

9.4 Working with Multiple Workbooks

You can open multiple workbooks in Excel and move between them by clicking on the workbook windows or using the keyboard shortcuts Ctrl+Tab (next workbook) and Ctrl+Shift+Tab (previous workbook).

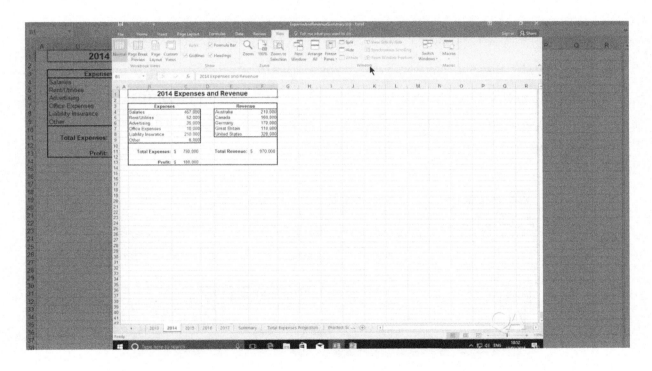

9.5 Referencing Cells in Other Workbooks

You can reference cells in other workbooks by using a formula that includes the workbook name enclosed in square brackets, the worksheet name, an exclamation mark, and the cell reference. For example, **=[Book2.xlsx]Sheet1!A1** refers to cell A1 in Sheet1 of Book2.xlsx.

9.6 Using 3D References

3D references allow you to reference the same cell or range in multiple worksheets. For example, **=SUM(Sheet1:Sheet3!A1)** adds the values in cell A1 from Sheet1, Sheet2, and Sheet3.

9.7 Consolidating Data

The Consolidate tool (under 'Data' tab > 'Data Tools' group > 'Consolidate') can be used to combine values from multiple ranges into one range. You can choose different consolidation methods like sum, average, count, etc.

9.8 Linking and Breaking Links

You can create links between workbooks to automatically update data across them. When you create a formula that references a cell in a different workbook, Excel creates a link to that workbook. When the data in the referenced cell changes, the formula updates automatically.

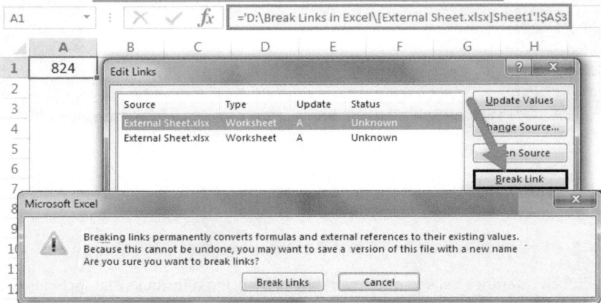

However, if you no longer need the data to update, you can break the link. To manage links, go to 'Data' tab > 'Connections' group > 'Edit Links'. Here, you can update, change, or break links.

9.9 Protecting Worksheets and Workbooks

To prevent unwanted changes to your worksheets or workbooks, you can protect them with a password. To protect a worksheet, go to 'Review' tab > 'Changes' group > 'Protect Sheet'. To protect a workbook, go to 'Review' tab > 'Changes' group > 'Protect Workbook'.

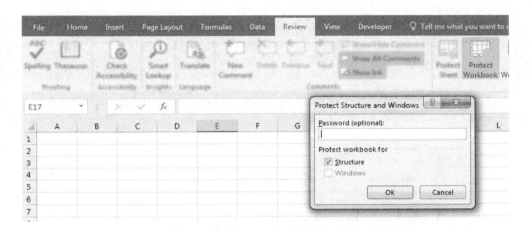

Remember, if you forget the password, you can't recover it. Be sure to keep a list of your passwords in a secure place.

9.10 Using the Watch Window

The Watch Window (under 'Formulas' tab > 'Formula Auditing' group > 'Watch Window') is a tool that lets you monitor the value, formula, and formatting of a cell even when you're working in a different worksheet or workbook. It's especially useful when you're working with large spreadsheets or multiple workbooks.

Chapter 10: Importing and Exporting Data in Excel

Excel provides several tools for importing data from and exporting data to different formats. This chapter will explain how to work with these tools and formats.

10.1 Importing Data from Text Files

You can import data from text files (like .txt or .csv) into Excel using the 'Text to Columns' tool (under 'Data' tab > 'Data Tools' group) or the 'Get External Data' group (under 'Data' tab).

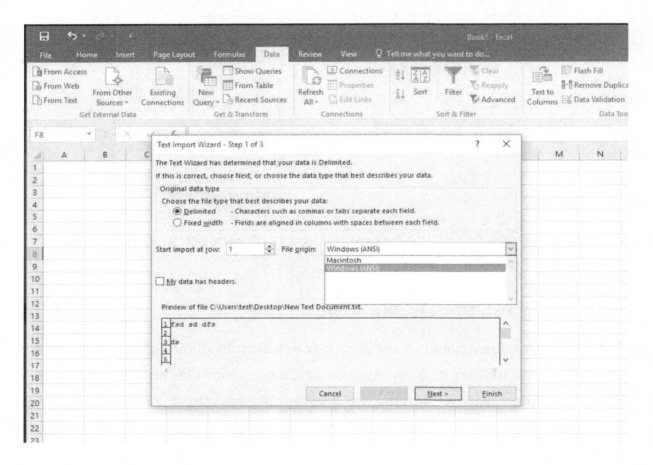

10.2 Importing Data from Databases

Excel can connect to various databases like SQL Server, Access, etc. To connect to a database, go to 'Data' tab > 'Get External Data' group > 'From Other Sources', and then select the type of database.

10.3 Importing Data from the Web

You can import data from a web page into Excel using the 'From Web' tool (under 'Data' tab > 'Get External Data' group). Just enter the URL of the web page, and Excel will import the data into a new worksheet.

10.4 Cleaning and Transforming Imported Data

After importing data, you may need to clean and transform it to make it useful. Excel provides many tools for this, like 'Text to Columns' (for splitting text into columns), 'Remove Duplicates' (for removing duplicate rows), and 'Flash Fill' (for automatically filling in values based on a pattern).

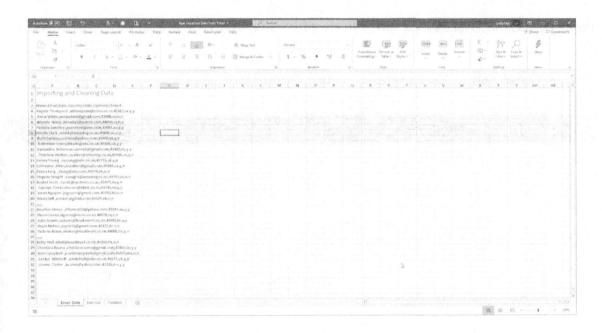

10.5 Exporting Data to Text Files

You can export data from Excel to a text file by going to 'File' > 'Save As' > 'Browse' and then choosing 'Text (Tab delimited)' or 'CSV (Comma delimited)' from the 'Save as type' drop-down list.

10.6 Exporting Data to PDF or XPS

To export your Excel workbook to a PDF or XPS file, go to 'File' > 'Export' > 'Create PDF/XPS'. You can choose to export the entire workbook, the active sheet, or a selected range.

10.7 Using Power Query to Import and Transform Data

Power Query is a powerful data connection technology that enables you to discover, connect, combine, and refine data across a wide variety of sources. With Power Query, you can filter and combine data from multiple sources, reshape it into a form that suits your needs, and then load it into Excel for further analysis.

10.8 Connecting to Data in the Cloud

With the rise of cloud computing, Excel has added functionality to connect to cloud-based data services like Microsoft's own Azure, SharePoint, or Dynamics 365, as well as third-party services like Salesforce. You can access these services via the 'Data' tab > 'Get Data' > 'From Online Services'.

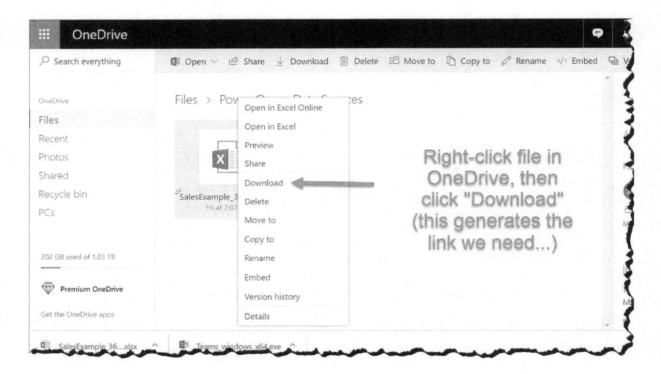

10.9 Importing and Analyzing XML and JSON Data

Excel also supports importing data from XML and JSON files, which are commonly used for data interchange in web services. You can import these files via the 'Data' tab > 'Get Data' > 'From File'.

Once you've imported XML or JSON data, Excel's rich feature set, including functions like **FILTERXML** and **WEBSERVICE**, and tools like Power Query, can be used to analyze this data.

```
http://localhost:8080/Json/SyncReply/Contacts
{
  - Contacts: [
      - {
          FirstName: "Demis",
          LastName: "Bellot",
          Email: "demis.bellot@gmail.com"
      },
      - {
          FirstName: "Steve",
          LastName: "Jobs",
          Email: "steve@apple.com"
      },
      - {
          FirstName: "Steve",
          LastName: "Ballmer",
          Email: "steve@microsoft.com"
      },
      - {
          FirstName: "Eric",
          LastName: "Schmidt",
          Email: "eric@google.com"
      },
      - {
          FirstName: "Larry",
          LastName: "Ellison",
          Email: "larry@oracle.com"
      }
  ]
}
```

```
http://localhost:8080/Xml/SyncReply/Contacts
<ContactsResponse xmlns:i="http://www.w3.org/20
    <Contacts>
        <Contact>
            <Email>demis.bellot@gmail.com</Email>
            <FirstName>Demis</FirstName>
            <LastName>Bellot</LastName>
        </Contact>
        <Contact>
            <Email>steve@apple.com</Email>
            <FirstName>Steve</FirstName>
            <LastName>Jobs</LastName>
        </Contact>
        <Contact>
            <Email>steve@microsoft.com</Email>
            <FirstName>Steve</FirstName>
            <LastName>Ballmer</LastName>
        </Contact>
        <Contact>
            <Email>eric@google.com</Email>
            <FirstName>Eric</FirstName>
            <LastName>Schmidt</LastName>
        </Contact>
        <Contact>
            <Email>larry@oracle.com</Email>
            <FirstName>Larry</FirstName>
            <LastName>Ellison</LastName>
        </Contact>
    </Contacts>
</ContactsResponse>
```

10.10 Exporting Excel Data to Other Office Applications

Excel data can be exported to other Office applications like Word and PowerPoint. For instance, you can copy a range of cells in Excel and paste it as a table in a Word document, or as a chart in a PowerPoint slide. Excel's 'Copy' and the other application's 'Paste' or 'Paste Special' commands can be used for these operations.

10.11 Converting Excel Files to Other Formats

Besides text files and PDF/XPS, Excel files can be saved in several other formats like OpenDocument Spreadsheet (.ods), Excel 97-2003 Workbook (.xls), and Excel Binary Workbook (.xlsb). Each format has its advantages and use cases.

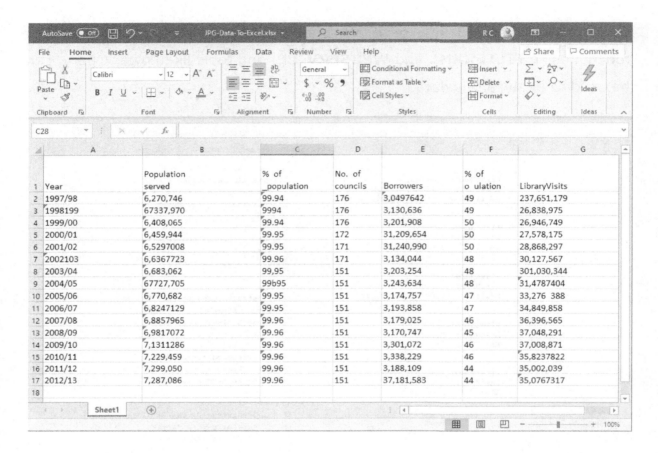

Year	Population served	% of population	No. of councils	Borrowers	% of o ulation	LibraryVisits
1997/98	6,270,746	99.94	176	3,0497642	49	237,651,179
1998199	67337,970	9994	176	3,130,636	49	26,838,975
1999/00	6,408,065	99.94	176	3,201,908	50	26,946,749
2000/01	6,459,944	99.95	172	31,209,654	50	27,578,175
2001/02	6,5297008	99.95	171	31,240,990	50	28,868,297
2002103	6,6367723	99.96	171	3,134,044	48	30,127,567
2003/04	6,683,062	99,95	151	3,203,254	48	301,030,344
2004/05	67727,705	99b95	151	3,243,634	48	31,4787404
2005/06	6,770,682	99.95	151	3,174,757	47	33,276 388
2006/07	6,8247129	99.95	151	3,193,858	47	34,849,858
2007/08	6,8857965	99.96	151	3,179,025	46	36,396,565
2008/09	6,9817072	99.96	151	3,170,747	45	37,048,291
2009/10	7,1311286	99.96	151	3,301,072	46	37,008,871
2010/11	7,229,459	99.96	151	3,338,229	46	35,8237822
2011/12	7,299,050	99,96	151	3,188,109	44	35,002,039
2012/13	7,287,086	99.96	151	37,181,583	44	35,0767317

Chapter 11: Data Analysis with Excel

Excel offers a wide range of tools for analyzing data, making it easier to draw conclusions and make decisions. This chapter will delve into the various data analysis features available in Excel.

11.1 Data Sorting and Filtering

Sorting data is a fundamental part of data analysis. It helps you to organize your data in a meaningful way. You can sort data in ascending or descending order by clicking on the 'Sort Ascending' or 'Sort Descending' buttons on the 'Data' tab. You can also sort by multiple columns by clicking 'Sort' and then adding levels to sort by.

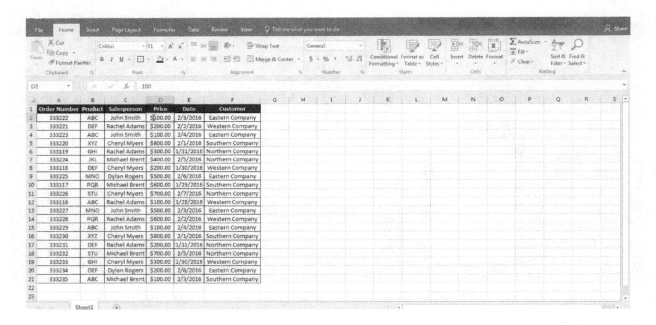

Filtering data, on the other hand, lets you view specific rows in your data without changing the order of the data. To filter data, you click the 'Filter' button on the 'Data' tab. This adds dropdowns to the headers of your data range, from which you can select the values you want to see.

11.2 Using Formulas for Data Analysis

Formulas in Excel are essential for analyzing data. They allow you to perform calculations and manipulate your data. There are numerous functions available for a variety of purposes, such as statistical functions (**AVERAGE**, **MEDIAN**, **MODE**, etc.), text functions (**LEFT**, **RIGHT**, **MID**, etc.), lookup functions (**VLOOKUP**, **HLOOKUP**, **INDEX**, **MATCH**, etc.), and logical functions (**IF**, **AND**, **OR**, etc.).

11.3 Conditional Formatting

Conditional formatting is a powerful tool in Excel that allows you to change the formatting of cells based on their values. You can highlight cells that meet certain criteria, create data bars, color scales, and icon sets. You can find the conditional formatting options under the 'Home' tab > 'Styles' group > 'Conditional Formatting'.

11.4 Data Validation

Data validation is a feature in Excel that allows you to control what kind of data can be entered into a cell. For example, you can restrict input to a certain range of numbers, a date within a specific range, or a list of options. You can set data validation rules by going to 'Data' tab > 'Data Tools' group > 'Data Validation'.

11.5 What-If Analysis

What-if analysis is a process that allows you to change the values in cells to see how those changes will affect the outcome of formulas on the sheet. Three kinds of what-if analysis tools come with Excel: scenarios, data tables, and goal seek.

- **Scenarios**: They allow you to swap out a set of values to see the effect on the result.
- **Data Tables**: They provide a shortcut for calculating multiple versions in one operation and a way to view and compare the results of all the different variations together on your worksheet.
- **Goal Seek**: It's a simple but powerful tool that works backward from the result to find an input value that will give you the result you want.

11.6 PivotTables and PivotCharts

PivotTables and PivotCharts are tools that allow you to summarize and analyze large data sets. They offer a way to "pivot" or rotate the data to view it from different perspectives. PivotTables can be created by selecting your data and then going to 'Insert' tab > 'Tables' group > 'PivotTable'. PivotCharts are created in a similar way but by clicking 'PivotChart' instead.

11.7 Advanced Filtering

For complex data sets, simple filtering might not be enough. Excel provides 'Advanced Filtering' which allows you to filter using complex criteria that can't be achieved with the regular Filter tool. You can find this option under 'Data' tab > 'Sort & Filter' group > 'Advanced'.

11.8 Analyzing Data with Excel Tables

Excel tables (which can be created under 'Insert' tab > 'Tables' group > 'Table') have several features that can help with data analysis. These features include automatic filtering and sorting, dynamically expanding ranges, structured references, and total rows. Each of these features can greatly aid in analyzing data.

11.9 Using Solver for Optimization Problems

Solver is an Excel add-in that can be used for optimization problems, like finding the best allocation of resources or the optimal solution to a problem. Solver works by changing a group of cells (the decision variables) to maximize, minimize, or achieve some target value for another cell (the objective cell), subject to certain constraints.

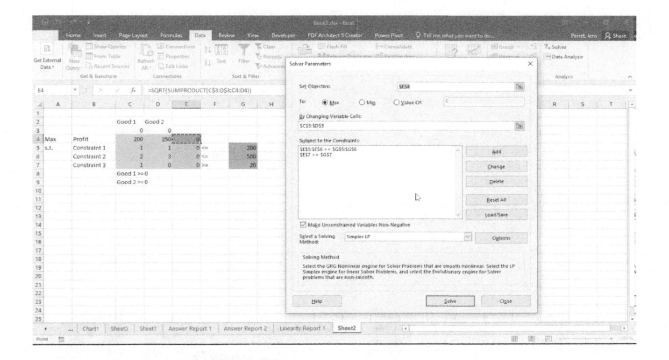

11.10 Data Analysis ToolPak

The Data Analysis ToolPak is an Excel add-in that provides data analysis tools for statistical and engineering analysis. The tools include descriptive statistics, histograms, correlation analysis, regression analysis, and more. You can enable the ToolPak under 'File' > 'Options' > 'Add-Ins'.

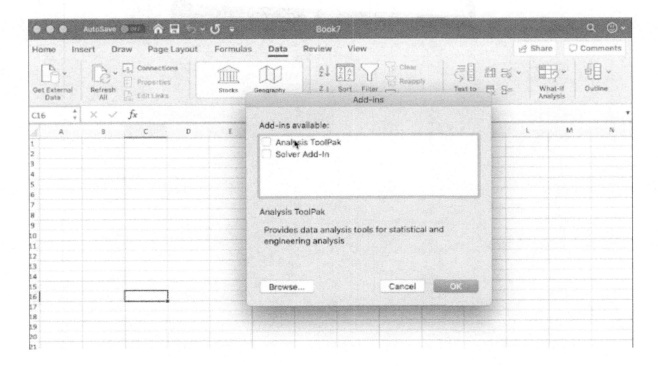

Chapter 12: Advanced Excel Features

Excel is packed with advanced features that can help you work more efficiently and effectively. This chapter will cover some of these features in detail.

12.1 Creating Macros with VBA

Excel includes a powerful programming language called Visual Basic for Applications (VBA). With VBA, you can automate repetitive tasks by creating macros. A macro is a sequence of instructions that Excel can execute automatically. Macros are created using the VBA editor, which you can open by pressing **Alt + F11**.

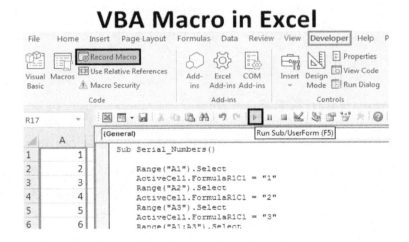

12.2 Understanding the Excel Object Model

The Excel Object Model is the structure Excel uses to represent the elements in a workbook. It consists of a hierarchy of objects, where each object represents something you can manipulate in Excel. For example, the Workbook object represents a workbook, the Worksheet object represents a worksheet, the Range object represents a cell or a range of cells, and so forth.

12.3 Working with UserForms

UserForms are custom user interface screens that you can develop in Excel using VBA. You can use UserForms to create custom dialogs, data entry forms, and navigation systems. A UserForm can contain various controls like text boxes, list boxes, combo boxes, option buttons, and others.

12.4 Error Handling in VBA

When you write VBA code, errors can occur. Error handling is the process of anticipating potential errors and writing your code in such a way that it can handle those errors gracefully. VBA provides several tools for error handling, such as the **On Error GoTo** statement, the **Err** object, and the **Debug** object.

12.5 Creating Custom Functions

In addition to Excel's built-in functions, you can create your own custom functions using VBA. These functions, also known as User Defined Functions (UDFs), can perform calculations or operations that are not available in the standard Excel functions.

12.6 Using Arrays in VBA

An array is a group of related data items that share a common name. Arrays can be very useful in VBA programming because they allow you to work with multiple values at once. VBA supports both one-dimensional and multi-dimensional arrays.

12.7 Working with Excel Events

Excel VBA allows you to write code that responds to certain events, such as a cell being changed or a workbook being opened. These events can be used to automate certain tasks or to customize Excel's behavior.

12.8 Automating Excel with Other Office Applications

Excel can interact with other Office applications like Word, PowerPoint, Outlook, and Access through VBA. For example, you can write VBA code in Excel to create a Word document, populate it with data from your Excel workbook, format the document, and save it.

12.9 Debugging VBA Code

Debugging is an essential part of writing and maintaining VBA code. Excel VBA includes several tools for debugging, such as the Immediate window and the Locals window. The Immediate window can be used to test snippets of code, while the Locals window can be used to inspect the values of variables while your code is running.

VBA Debug Print

```
Sub VBA_Debug1()
    Debug.Print "This is how Debug Print works!!"
End Sub

Sub VBA_Debug2()

    Dim A As Integer
    Dim B As Double
    Dim C As Long
A = 1
B = 123.123
C = 123123123
Debug.Print A
Debug.Print B
```

Immediate

```
This is how Debug Print works!!

1
123.123
123123123
```

12.10 Controlling Program Flow

VBA provides several statements that allow you to control the flow of your program. These include conditional statements like **If...Then...Else**, loop statements like **For...Next** and **Do...Loop**, and jump statements like **GoTo**.

12.11 Working with Text Files

VBA includes functions for working with text files. For example, you can write a macro that reads data from a text file into an Excel worksheet or writes data from a worksheet into a text file. The **Open** statement can be used to open a file, the **Line Input** statement can be used to read a line of text from a file, and the **Print** statement can be used to write to a file.

12.12 Using the Windows API

The Windows API (Application Programming Interface) is a set of functions and procedures that are part of the Windows operating system. These functions and procedures can be called from VBA code to perform tasks that are not directly supported by VBA. However, be aware that using the Windows API requires a good understanding of programming and the Windows operating system.

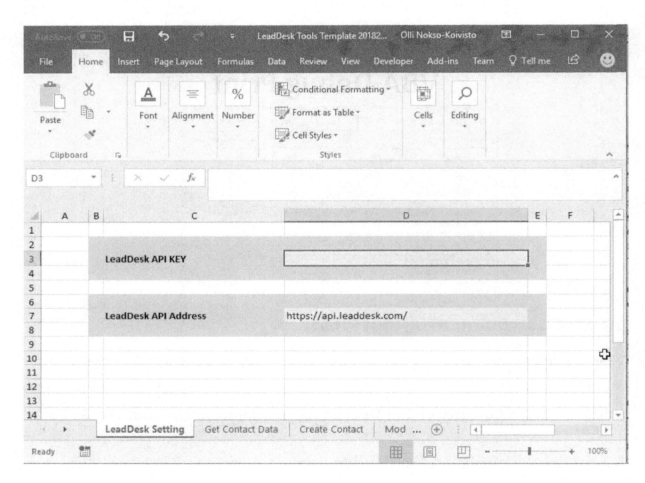

Excel is a powerful tool that can assist with various business and financial tasks. This chapter will delve into the ways in which Excel can be used in a business and finance context.

13.1 Financial Functions

Excel offers a variety of built-in financial functions that can be used to perform complex financial calculations. Functions such as **PMT** (calculates the payment for a loan based on constant payments and a constant interest rate), **FV** (returns the future value of an investment), **NPV** (returns the net present value of an investment based on a series of periodic cash flows and a discount rate), and **IRR** (returns the internal rate of return for a series of periodic cash flows) can be of great use in financial modeling and analysis.

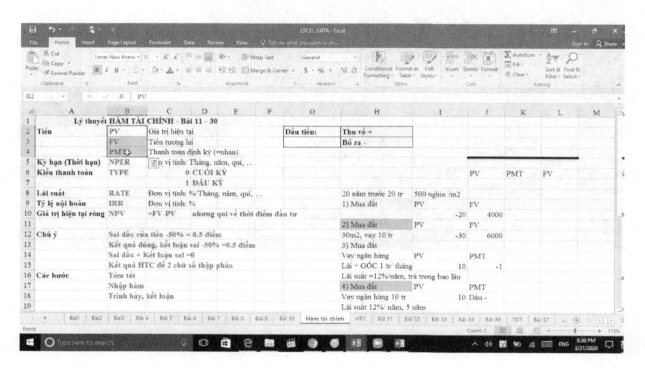

13.2 Investment Analysis

Investment analysis is an essential part of financial planning and decision making. Excel can assist with various aspects of investment analysis. You can use Excel to calculate investment returns, analyze portfolio performance, assess risks, and make investment decisions.

13.3 Creating Business Models

Business modeling involves creating a theoretical model to represent the structure and behavior of a business. Excel is a useful tool for creating business models. You can use Excel to create financial models, operational models, strategic models, and other types of business models.

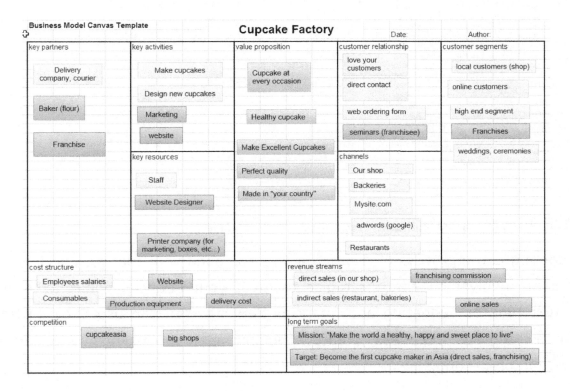

13.4 Financial Reporting

Financial reporting involves the preparation of financial documents that disclose an organization's financial status to management, investors, and the government. Excel is commonly used in financial reporting to create income statements, balance sheets, cash flow statements, and other financial reports.

13.5 Sales Forecasting

Sales forecasting is the process of estimating future sales. Accurate sales forecasts enable businesses to make informed business decisions and predict short-term and long-term performance. Excel can be used to create sales forecasts using historical sales data and various forecasting methods, such as linear regression, moving averages, and exponential smoothing.

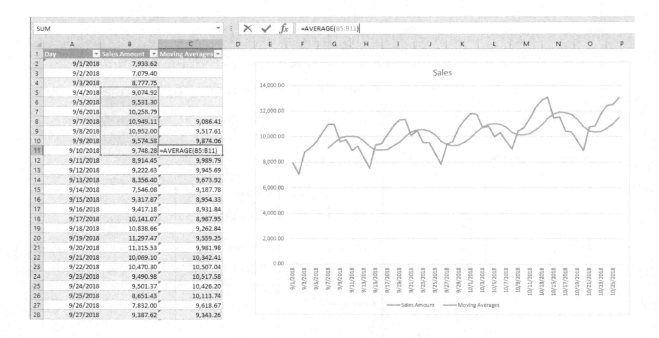

13.6 Budgeting and Financial Planning

Budgeting is the process of creating a plan to spend your money, and financial planning involves making strategies to meet your financial goals. Excel is a popular tool for budgeting and financial planning. You can use Excel to track your income and expenses, create a budget, plan for savings, and perform financial forecasting.

PERSONAL MONTHLY BUDGET

SUMMARY

Income	$	7,257.00
Savings Goal	$	1,655.00
Expenses	$	5,359.00
POTENTIAL TO SAVE	**$**	**243.00**

Enter Income, Savings, and Expense Data, below. Overview information above will generate automatically.

	JAN	FEB	MAR	APR	MAY	JUN	JUL	AUG	SEPT	OCT	NOV	DEC	Total
INCOME													
Salary/Wages	$ 5,987.00												$ 5,987.00
Interest Income	$ 200.00												$ 200.00
Dividends	$ 100.00												$ 100.00
Refunds/Reimbursements	$ 55.00												$ 55.00
Business	$ 500.00												$ 500.00
Pension	$ 300.00												$ 300.00
Misc.	$ 115.00												$ 115.00
TOTAL	$ 7,257.00	$ -	$ -	$ -	$ -	$ -	$ -	$ -	$ -	$ -	$ -	$ -	$ 7,257.00
SAVINGS													
Emergency Fund	$ 500.00	$ -	$ -	$ -	$ -	$ -	$ -	$ -	$ -	$ -	$ -	$ -	500.00
Transfer to Savings	$ 200.00	$ -	$ -	$ -	$ -	$ -	$ -	$ -	$ -	$ -	$ -	$ -	200.00
Retirement(401K, IRA)	$ 100.00	$ -	$ -	$ -	$ -	$ -	$ -	$ -	$ -	$ -	$ -	$ -	100.00
Investments	$ 55.00	$ -	$ -	$ -	$ -	$ -	$ -	$ -	$ -	$ -	$ -	$ -	55.00
Education	$ 500.00	$ -	$ -	$ -	$ -	$ -	$ -	$ -	$ -	$ -	$ -	$ -	500.00
Other	$ 300.00	$ -	$ -	$ -	$ -	$ -	$ -	$ -	$ -	$ -	$ -	$ -	300.00
TOTAL	$ 1,655.00	$ -	$ -	$ -	$ -	$ -	$ -	$ -	$ -	$ -	$ -	$ -	1,655.00
EXPENSES													
HOME													
Mortgage/rent	$ 2,250.00	$ -	$ -	$ -	$ -	$ -	$ -	$ -	$ -	$ -	$ -	$ -	2,250.00
Home/Rental Insurance	$ 25.00	$ -	$ -	$ -	$ -	$ -	$ -	$ -	$ -	$ -	$ -	$ -	25.00
Electricity	$ 40.00	$ -	$ -	$ -	$ -	$ -	$ -	$ -	$ -	$ -	$ -	$ -	40.00
Gas/Oil	$ 44.00	$ -	$ -	$ -	$ -	$ -	$ -	$ -	$ -	$ -	$ -	$ -	44.00
Water/Sewer/Trash	$ 20.00	$ -	$ -	$ -	$ -	$ -	$ -	$ -	$ -	$ -	$ -	$ -	20.00
Phone	$ 15.00	$ -	$ -	$ -	$ -	$ -	$ -	$ -	$ -	$ -	$ -	$ -	15.00
Cable/Satellite	$ -	$ -	$ -	$ -	$ -	$ -	$ -	$ -	$ -	$ -	$ -	$ -	-
Internet	$ 29.00	$ -	$ -	$ -	$ -	$ -	$ -	$ -	$ -	$ -	$ -	$ -	29.00
Furnishing/Appliances	$ -	$ -	$ -	$ -	$ -	$ -	$ -	$ -	$ -	$ -	$ -	$ -	-
Lawn/Garden													

13.7 Risk Analysis

Risk analysis involves identifying and assessing factors that could negatively affect key business initiatives or projects. Excel provides tools for conducting risk analysis. For instance, you can use the **Data Analysis** tool pack to carry out a simulation or "What-if" analysis to evaluate risks.

13.8 Project Management

Excel can be a valuable tool for project management. With Excel, you can create project schedules, allocate resources, track project progress, and generate project reports. For instance, a Gantt chart, which visualizes project tasks over a timeline, can easily be created in Excel.

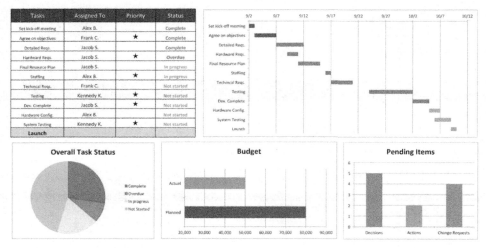

Smartsheet Sights™ give your team the ability to work smarter, with visibility into work as it's getting done

13.9 Inventory Management

Inventory management involves overseeing the flow of items into and out of your stock. It's crucial for businesses to have enough inventory to meet customer demand but not so much that you waste resources storing it. Excel can assist in managing inventory with features like tables for tracking, formulas for automatic calculations, and pivot tables for easy data analysis.

13.10 Data Validation

Data validation is an Excel feature that you can use to control what kind of information is entered into a cell. For example, you can set up data validation to prevent users from entering text in a cell that requires a date or prevent numbers outside a specific range. This is particularly useful in a business context where data accuracy is critical.

13.11 Advanced Excel Charts

Excel has a broad array of advanced charting capabilities which can be effectively used for business presentations and analysis. These include Waterfall charts, which are great for understanding cumulative effects of sequential positive or negative values; and Sunburst charts, which can visually represent hierarchical data across two dimensions, shown in concentric rings where each ring represents a level in the hierarchy.

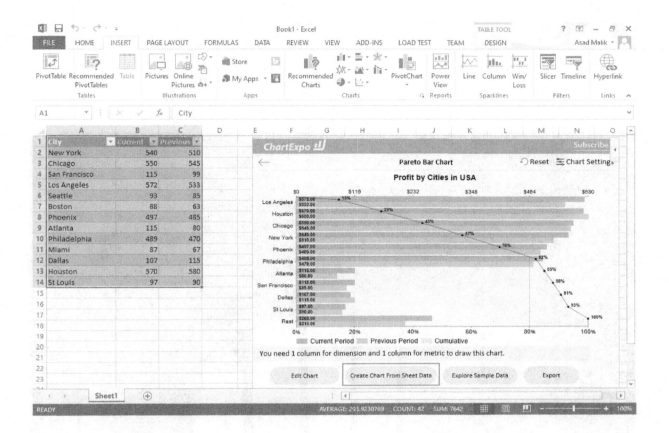

13.12 Solving Complex Problems with Solver

Solver is a what-if analysis tool for optimization in Excel. You can use Solver to find an optimal (maximum or minimum) value for a formula in one cell, subject to constraints or limits on the values of other formula cells. In a business context, Solver can be used for resource allocation or for performing goal seek operations.

Chapter 14: Data Analysis with Excel

Data analysis is an integral part of decision making in business and research. Excel is a versatile tool that provides several features to facilitate extensive data analysis. This chapter will cover some of these features.

14.1 Excel Tables

Excel tables are a powerful tool to manage and analyze a group of related data. You can sort and filter data in tables, apply formula-based formatting and styles, and create calculated columns for more complex calculations.

14.2 Advanced Filtering

Advanced filtering is a technique in Excel to filter for multiple conditions or if your auto filter has a limitation. You can use complex criteria to filter for specific information, and you can even use formulas as your criteria.

14.3 PivotTables

PivotTables are one of Excel's most powerful data-analysis tools. They are used to summarize, analyze, explore, and present summary data. PivotTables make it easy to arrange and pivot statistics in order to draw further insights from data.

14.4 Data Validation and Data Cleaning

Data validation is an Excel feature that you can use to define restrictions on what data can or should be entered in a cell. You can customize the criteria for all types of data, including text, date, time, and numbers. Furthermore, data cleaning is crucial to ensure the accuracy of the analysis. It involves dealing with missing values, duplicates, or incorrect data types.

14.5 Using Statistical Functions

Excel provides a wide range of statistical functions, including **AVERAGE**, **MEDIAN**, **MODE**, **STDEV**, **VAR**, and many others. These functions can be used to perform statistical analysis on sets of data.

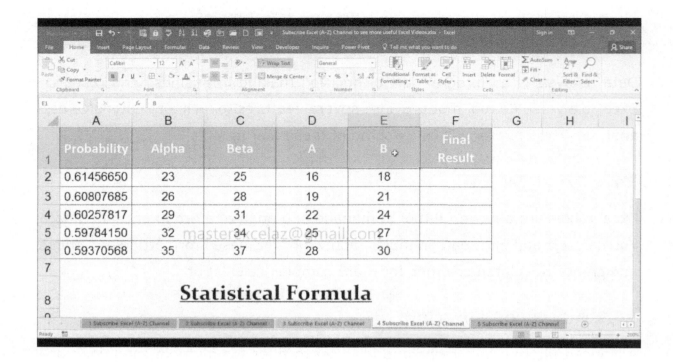

Probability	Alpha	Beta	A	B	Final Result
0.61456650	23	25	16	18	
0.60807685	26	28	19	21	
0.60257817	29	31	22	24	
0.59784150	32	34	25	27	
0.59370568	35	37	28	30	

Statistical Formula

14.6 Using Excel's Analysis ToolPak

The Analysis ToolPak is an Excel add-in program that provides data analysis tools for statistical and engineering analysis. It can be used to perform complex analyses like regression analysis, paired t-tests, and Fourier analysis.

14.7 Power Query for Data Transformation

Power Query is a data connection technology that enables you to discover, connect, combine, and refine data across a wide variety of sources. You can easily shape and transform data from various sources and load it into an Excel worksheet or Power Pivot window to create compelling data models.

14.8 Power Pivot for Data Modeling

Power Pivot is an Excel add-in you can use to perform powerful data analysis and create sophisticated data models. By using Power Pivot for Excel, you can transform enormous quantities of data with incredible speed into meaningful information to get the answers you need in seconds.

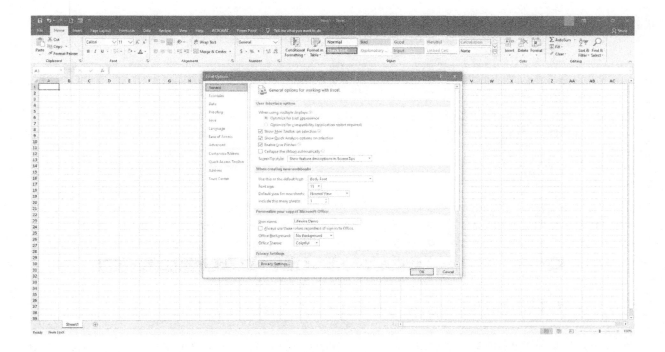

14.9 Data Visualization with Charts and Graphs

Data visualization is a crucial part of data analysis. Excel provides a variety of chart types, such as line charts, bar charts, pie charts, scatter plots, and more, which can be used to represent data and highlight trends and patterns visually.

14.10 Conditional Formatting for Data Analysis

Conditional formatting is a powerful feature in Excel that allows you to change the format of cells based on their contents. For example, you might use a color scale to highlight a range of values, or a data bar to visually represent numerical values.

14.11 Excel Formulas for Data Analysis

Excel has a vast library of built-in formulas that you can use for data analysis. These include lookup and reference functions, mathematical functions, text functions, and date and time functions, among others.

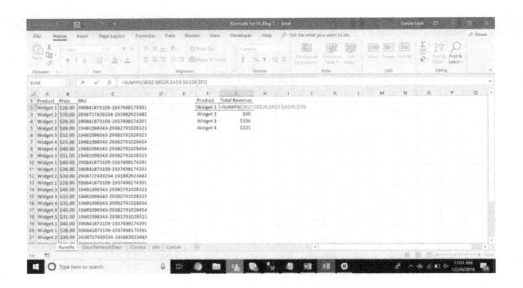

14.12 Using Slicers and Timelines with PivotTables

Slicers and timelines are visual filters. With slicers, you can filter your data in a PivotTable or PivotChart more intuitively. You can see the current filter state without having to open drop-down lists, which makes it easy to understand what exactly is shown in your PivotTable or PivotChart.

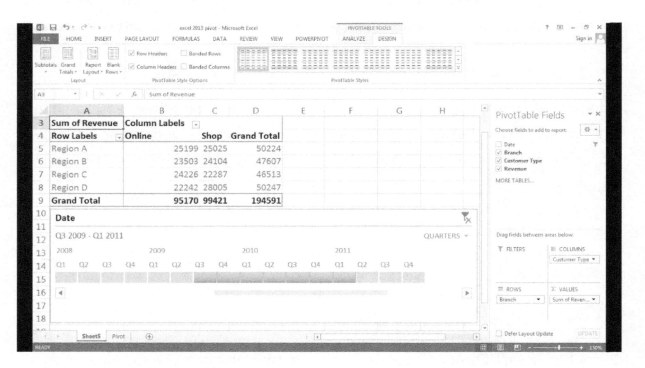

Excel VBA

Chapter 15: Excel VBA and Macros

Excel's VBA (Visual Basic for Applications) is a powerful feature that enables automation of tasks in Excel. Macros are sequences of instructions that automate Excel, and they're written in VBA. This chapter will guide you through the basics of VBA and Macros.

15.1 Understanding VBA

VBA is a programming language developed by Microsoft —used in Excel to automate tasks. If there's an activity you have to do repeatedly, you can record it in a macro and then just replay it when you need it.

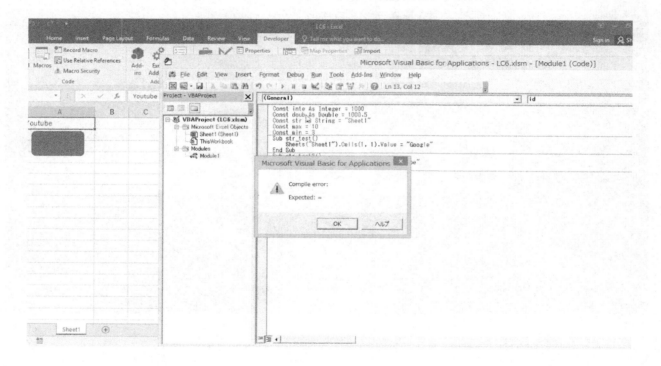

15.2 Introduction to Macros

Macros are programs in VBA created to automate tasks. Excel provides a feature to record the task you perform using Excel options and then save it as a macro. You can then run the recorded steps without typing the whole steps again.

15.3 Recording Macros

Excel allows you to record a sequence of tasks in the form of a macro and then execute those tasks all at once, as many times as you like. This section will cover how to record a macro, where to store a macro, and how to run a macro.

15.4 Writing VBA Code

While recording a macro can automate a lot of tasks, it might not be efficient or entirely suited to your specific needs. Writing your own VBA code allows you to create more complex and customized solutions. This section would cover the basics of writing VBA code, understanding the VBA editor, and using basic VBA elements like variables, loops, and conditional statements.

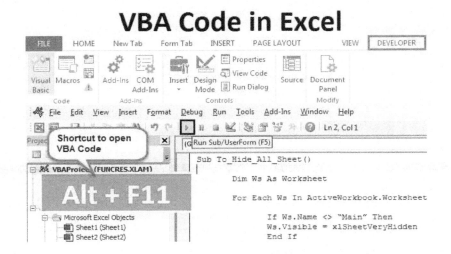

15.5 Debugging and Error Handling

When writing VBA code, you'll inevitably run into errors and bugs. Debugging involves identifying and fixing these errors, and error handling is the process of anticipating potential errors and determining how your program should respond to them.

15.6 User-Defined Functions (UDFs)

User-Defined Functions (UDFs) are functions created by the user that are not part of Excel's built-in suite of functions. They can be used to simplify code and improve efficiency.

15.7 Creating Interactive Userforms

Userforms are custom user interface screens that you can develop in Excel VBA to interact with the users of your Excel programs. Userforms are useful for getting a small amount of input from the user and providing interactive feedback based on that input.

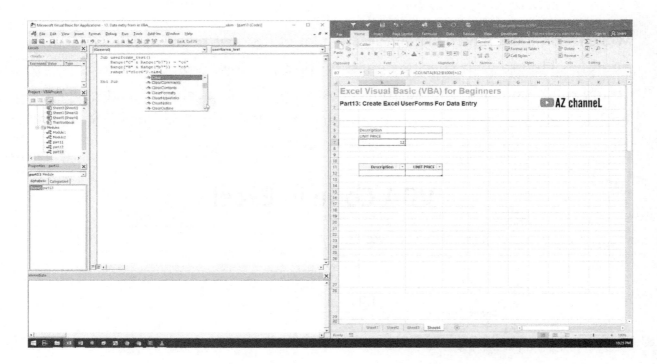

15.8 Advanced VBA Techniques

As you get more comfortable with VBA, there are more advanced techniques that can further enhance your macros. This includes working with arrays, collections, and dictionaries, understanding event-driven programming, and using API calls for more complex tasks.

15.9 Security and Protection in VBA

Understanding security and protection in VBA is crucial to protect your code and your data. This includes learning how to protect your VBA code from unauthorized access and how to prevent security risks from macros.

15.10 Automating Excel with VBA

Once you've learned the basics of VBA, you can start to automate many of your Excel tasks. This could include creating reports, cleaning data, or updating values. The possibilities are endless with VBA.

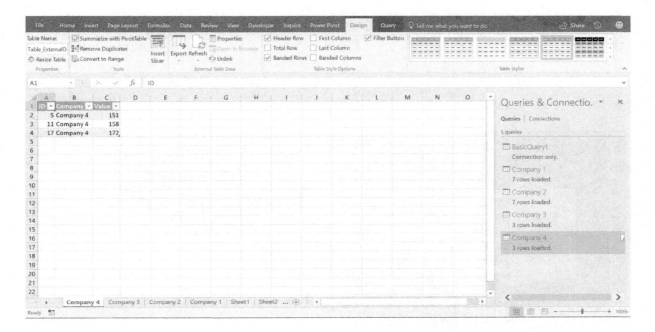

15.11 Interacting with Other Applications through VBA

VBA isn't just limited to Excel - you can use it to control other Microsoft Office applications, such as Word, PowerPoint, and Access. This can be incredibly useful for tasks that require you to work across multiple applications.

15.12 Best Practices in VBA Programming

As with any programming language, there are best practices in VBA that can help ensure your code is clean, efficient, and easy to understand. This includes tips for structuring your code, naming conventions, and error handling.

Chapter 16: Excel and Power BI

Power BI is a suite of business analytics tools that can deliver insights from your data. It provides interactive visualizations with self-service business intelligence capabilities. This chapter will guide you on how to use Excel with Power BI.

16.1 Understanding Power BI

Power BI is a collection of software services, apps, and connectors that combine to turn your unrelated data sources into coherent, visually immersive, and interactive insights.

16.2 Power BI and Excel: The Perfect Pair

Excel and Power BI are designed to work together. This is great news for businesses that are already data-oriented and are using Excel. It's easy to move data back and forth between Excel and Power BI, this section would explain how.

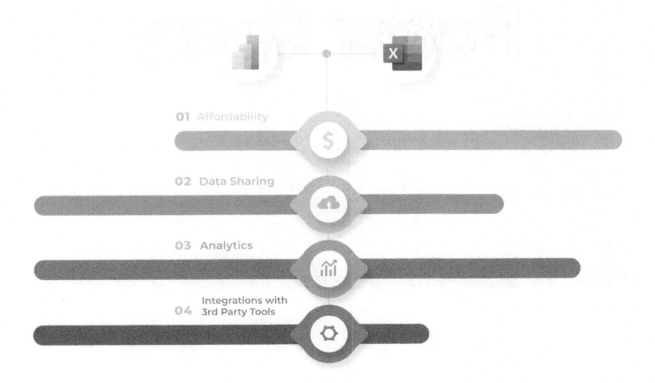

01 Affordability

02 Data Sharing

03 Analytics

04 Integrations with 3rd Party Tools

16.3 Importing Excel Data into Power BI

Power BI lets you easily import Excel workbooks and use them as a data source. This section would guide readers on how to import data from Excel into Power BI, transform it into a data model, and visualize it using Power BI tools.

16.4 Power Query in Power BI

Power Query is a powerful tool used in Power BI to perform complex transformations on your data before it is loaded into your data model. It can connect to various sources, providing an intuitive interface for transforming and cleaning your data.

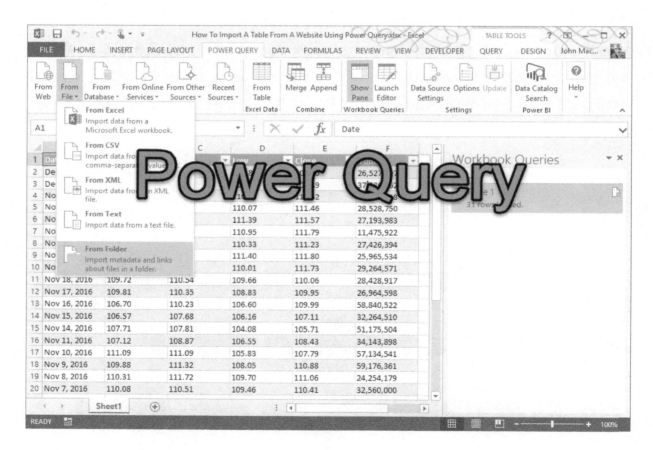

16.5 Creating Reports in Power BI

Once your data is imported into Power BI, you can create interactive reports and dashboards. This section would cover the basics of creating a report, adding visuals, and customizing your report layout.

16.6 Publishing and Sharing Reports

Once you've created a report, you can publish it to the Power BI service, where you can create dashboards, share your reports with others, and access them from anywhere using Power BI mobile.

16.7 Power BI and Excel: Working Together

The power of Power BI lies in its integration with other Microsoft products like Excel. Learn how to pin Excel visuals in your Power BI dashboards, how to connect Excel to Power BI datasets, and how to use Power BI data in Excel.

16.8 Power BI Desktop vs Power BI Service

Power BI Desktop is a Windows application for desktop computers, and Power BI Service is an online SaaS (Software as a Service) service. This section will compare and contrast the two to help users understand when to use which tool.

16.9 Advanced Data Transformations in Power Query

While we've covered the basics of Power Query, it's a tool with a lot of depth. In this section, we could discuss more advanced transformations such as merging queries, grouping data, and using the advanced editor.

16.10 Creating and Managing Dataflows

Dataflows are a type of data preparation that are reusable across multiple Power BI reports and dashboards. They simplify the process of transforming data, and they are stored in the cloud for easy access and management.

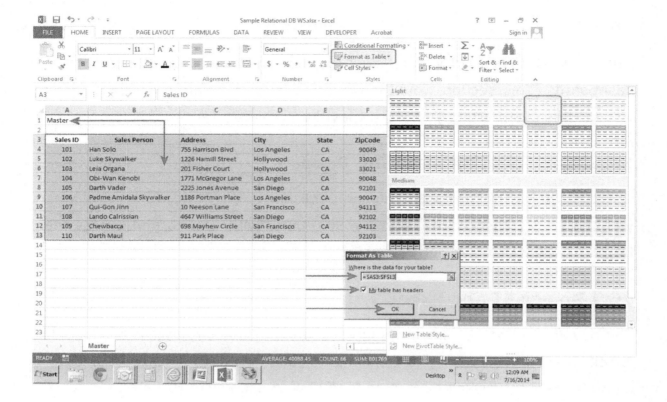

16.11 Using DAX in Power BI

Data Analysis Expressions (DAX) is a formula language used in Power BI. DAX can be used to create new information from data already in your model and to aggregate, calculate and analyse data in different ways.

16.12 Tips and Tricks for Power BI

Every tool has its tricks and hidden features, and Power BI is no exception. This section will provide tips and tricks to make readers more efficient and effective when using Power BI.

Conclusion: Mastering Excel 2023 and Beyond

You've made it! You've journeyed through the depths of Excel 2023, from the most basic functions to the advanced features that make Excel the powerhouse that it is. You've explored everything from data entry and basic formulas to data analysis, visualization, VBA automation, and even Power BI integration.

But remember, the true strength of Excel lies not just in knowing these features, but in understanding how to combine them to solve real-world problems. Whether you're analyzing business data, managing budgets, or trying to uncover insights from complex datasets, Excel is a tool that can help you do it all.

So what's next?

Excel, like any tool, is continuously evolving. With each new version, Microsoft adds new features and enhances existing ones, always aiming to make the software more powerful and easier to use. Stay current with these changes. Participate in forums, read blogs, and don't be afraid to experiment with new features and techniques.

Remember, this book is not the end of your Excel journey; it's just the beginning. Real learning happens when you apply what you've learned to your projects. Don't be afraid to experiment, make mistakes, and learn from them. That's the path to mastery.

In the ever-changing landscape of data, Excel continues to be a reliable constant. With the foundation you've built from this book, you are well-equipped to use Excel 2023 to its full potential and adapt to whatever changes future versions may bring.

Thank you for taking this journey through Excel 2023 with us. Keep exploring, keep learning, and most importantly, keep excelling!

LEAVE A REVIEW & GET REWARDED!

Don't wait! Scan the QR Code and **CLAIM YOUR EXCLUSIVE FREE BONUSES!**

Made in United States
North Haven, CT
02 March 2024

49190583R00063